The
Weekend
Baker

# PAUL HOLLYWOOD

# The Weekend Baker

PHOTOGRAPHY BY ISSY CROKER

MICHAEL JOSEPH
*an imprint of*
Penguin Books

**TO MY SON JOSH**

MICHAEL JOSEPH

UK | USA | Canada | Ireland | Australia
India | New Zealand | South Africa

Michael Joseph is part of the Penguin Random House group of companies
whose addresses can be found at global.penguinrandomhouse.com.

Penguin
Random House
UK

First published 2016

001

Text copyright © Paul Hollywood, 2016
Photography copyright © Issy Croker, 2016
Additional photography copyright © Dunk Barnes/Reef TV Ltd, 2016 and as follows:
45 © Mariusz Kluzniak/Getty Images; 46–7 © Steve Ryan/Getty; 164–5 © Seb Oliver/Getty
Images; 166–7 © Westend61/Getty images; 172 (L-R) © Pat Behnke/Alamy; © Mr Doomits/
Alamy; © Bloomberg/Contributor/Getty; © Michael Zegers/LOOK-foto/Getty Images; ©
travelgame/Getty Images; © John Freeman/Getty Images; © filmfoto-03edit/Alamy; © Danita
Delimont/Getty Images; © EURASIA PRESS/Getty Images; 182 © imageBROKER/Alamy
Stock Photo; 219 © Diego Lezama/Getty Images; 220–21 © THEPALMER/Getty Images;
234–5 © AGF/Contributor/Getty; 239 © Cultura RM Exclusive/Philip Lee Harvey/Getty
Images; 240–41 © Carlos De Toro/Getty Images; 249 © Kasia Nowak/Alamy Stock Photo
and © Gregory King/Alamy Stock Photo; 257 © Richard Nowitz/Getty Images; 258–9 ©
rusm/Getty Images

The 'Casatiello' recipe on page 58 is taken from *Passione* by Gennaro Contaldo;
copyright © Gennaro Contaldo, 2003; reproduced by permission
of the Headline Publishing Group.

The moral right of the copyright holders has been asserted

Colour reproduction by Altaimage Ltd
Printed in Italy by Graphicom S.r.l

A CIP catalogue record for this book is available from the British Library

ISBN: 978–0–718–18401–8
www.greenpenguin.co.uk

MIX
Paper from
responsible sources
FSC
www.fsc.org    FSC® C018179

Penguin Random House is committed to a
sustainable future for our business, our readers
and our planet. This book is made from Forest
Stewardship Council® certified paper.

# CONTENTS

# INTRODUCTION

'FOR ME, LOOKING AT IT IN ITS SIMPLEST FORM, OUR CULTURES ARE COMPLETELY BASED ON BAKING, AND YOU CAN SEE THAT THROUGHOUT THE WORLD. **FLOUR IS THE UNIFYING FACTOR** – THE BASE FOOD IN SO MANY CULTURES.'

I have wanted to write this book for a long time. It sees me discovering baking cultures of the world in ten of its most amazing cities, some of which I'd never been to before or didn't know a great deal about. So it was a chance for me to take a few weekend breaks and just explore. I wasn't sure what each place would offer me in terms of exciting discoveries, but the experience will stay with me for ever.

I have been around baking all my life and what these trips and this journey gave back to me was a huge slice of passion for what I do. I'm not saying that I had forgotten things or techniques, but it opened my eyes to just how important baking is to people all over the world, from Cubans in Miami – a relatively new city – to those who love a traditional British afternoon tea; from the third and fourth generations of family-run bakeries in Poland to the migrants who settled in the USA and developed a new style of baking unique to New York (with a nod to their places of origin). And then there's Copenhagen – I've made so many Danish pastries over the years, so to travel to where they celebrate them more than anywhere else in the world was just amazing. They produce some of the best Danish pastries I've ever tasted, giving them twists like adding wholemeal flour to the dough. I'd never tried this before, but it tastes so much better.

For me, looking at it in its simplest form, our cultures are completely based on baking, and you can see that throughout the world. Flour is the unifying factor – the base food in so many cultures. Even in those places that I thought would be so different from the UK, like Russia. Have a look at the beautiful design of the Russian pies on page 263. The presentation might be very different, but the beef pie is basically a massive sausage roll and it took me straight back to Britain when I tasted it.

MY EYES WERE OPENED TO JUST HOW IMPORTANT
BAKING IS TO PEOPLE ALL OVER THE WORLD

Throughout my career, I always used the word 'pizza' flippantly – until I met Enzo Coccia in Naples. I honestly learnt more in an afternoon with him then I have in the last 49 years of eating pizza. Before I went, I thought I knew how to make pizza, but listening to Enzo I realised I didn't. He signed a book to me and called me 'pizzaiolo', which means 'novice pizza-maker', on the bottom rung of a huge ladder; and there was me thinking I was a pizza-maker already…

One of the things that was really fascinating for me on these trips was meeting people from all over the world who share my passion for baking. Like Jim Lahey in New York, who has developed a style of baking that has made him an internet success – the 'no-knead bread'. I don't want to hear any of those 'I haven't got the time' excuses any more! His method blows all of that out of the water and it means you can easily make bread at home, whether you are time-poor or not. Have a look at page 209.

Meeting people like Jim, who love their job and carry a torch for baking, was definitely a high point for me. I've kept in touch with all of the people I met and am definitely going to return to several of the places this year to visit them again. I'm currently thinking of more cities I'd like to visit to expand my knowledge of baking even further, and I look forward to meeting the bakers who are carving out some truly unique bakes.

All the cities I visited in this book are very easy to get to. The furthest away is Miami (9 hours on a plane), but some are only an hour away. If you have a spare weekend and want to check out some of these places, then take the book and do it. I loved the energy and vibe in Miami – an energy I hadn't seen before, coming from a whole mix of cultures – where they have created their own baking repertoire. New York is 6 hours by plane, or a very long swim. They don't call it the Big Apple for nothing; it is a massive place. But dig a bit deeper and you will find little local bakeries on the corners serving some of the best things you'll ever eat. Don't let Russia scare you. Some of the stereotypes are true (yes, they do all drive Ladas!) but St Petersburg is, without a doubt, the prettiest place I've ever been to in my life. Three hours away on a plane – you'll adore it. The people, the place and the bakes are all very special. A quick jaunt across the Channel to Paris, the chic home of the croissant and baguette, is another perfect place for a weekend break to discover some weekend bakes.

What I think is interesting is that there are about twenty base recipes, in my view, that have branched out across the world, and all baking stems from them. Look at fruit cake, for instance. The idea of putting fruit into something you bake has been around for thousands of years and different countries have different ways of making or serving it. Add yeast to it and it becomes a risen dough, whether a hot cross bun or afternoon teacake in Britain, a risen fruit bread in France or a dumpling in Poland.

When it comes to the recipes in this book, don't be scared of them because of how many stages they have or how complicated they look. Each stage is easily broken down so you can take your time. There are some simpler recipes for you to try first and some more challenging ones for you to move on to. It's like making a casserole that takes a long time to cook but only minutes to prepare. So please don't look at the prove time and think, 'I'm not doing it as it's 24 hours work.' It's not! The recipes are very quick to prepare and, at the end, you'll have made something very special because you've given it the time it needs to prove or do its thing properly. Overall, I would say don't try to change or upscale the recipes from the off. Master them first and then you can bring your own tweaks into play, like if you want more fruit or cheese or meat then do it, but master my way first – walk before you can run.

One thing I found on my travels is that baking is very much a family thing – a lot of the recipes have been passed down from generation to generation and legends have formed. In Warsaw I visited a bakery where a young man had hidden from the Nazis in a warm baking pit in the ground. They didn't catch him; he ended up working there and now it is run by his great-grandsons. At Junior's in Brooklyn, the grandson of the original owner has carried on his grandfather's good work and created one of the best cheesecake brands in America. It just proves the point that if you create a good bake, people will come. So find your new signature bake and friends and family will want to come to your house to eat. All recipes are formed from someone's idea and home baking is the key to keeping these recipes alive. This is why I want to pass some of my recipes down to you, so you can pass them on to your families.

# SUN BAKED /

## MADRID

Churros / Spanish hot chocolate / Chocolate-dipped palmiers /
Ibérico ham and manchego empanada / Orange and almond empanada /
Roscón de reyes / Spanish sable biscuits / Buñuelos de viento /
Squid ink and sweet pepper bread / Torta

As Madrid is Spain's political, economic and cultural centre, it's easy to see why it's the country's most visited city. Carefully preserved historic neighbourhoods and streets are hidden amongst its thriving modern infrastructure and towering skyscrapers – Madrid truly is a city of contrast and perfect for a weekend away.

Walking through these streets you'll find an abundance of cafés, bakeries and restaurants, many upholding the traditional flavours and delicacies that make up this city's rich cultural heritage. The Antigua Pastelería del Pozo, for example, a charming deli cum bakery, is Madrid's oldest bakery and most famous for its *roscón de reyes*. Leal, the owner, whose grandfather bought the shop in the 1920s, showed me their unique technique for making this Spanish delicacy: a ring-shaped, yellow sweet bread topped with sugared fruit (see page 31 for my version). It's something to try any time of year, although it is particularly well suited to the festive season due to its sheer extravagance – truly a bake fit for a king.

I couldn't visit Madrid without trying the traditional Spanish sweet treat *churros*, and where better to do so than at the world-famous Chocolatería San Ginés – a beautiful nineteenth-century inn. It's not hard to see why locals and tourists flock to this deli when you taste chef Delphi Artiñano's recipe with a rich helping of hot chocolate, the perfect accompaniment (see pages 17 and 18).

Who better to guide me through some of the city's favourite dishes than my old friend and Madrid native, Omar Allibhoy. We wandered through vibrant markets together and Omar showed me his favourite recipe for *buñuelos de viento* – light, fluffy fritters traditionally baked to celebrate All Saints' Day. You'll find these on page 34. I also have Omar to thank for recommending that I visit Horno de San Onofre, owned by chef Daniel Guerrero. Daniel's food is inspired by Spain's fusion of Arab and Christian cultures and it was a pleasure to cook *empanadas* – pastry turnovers stuffed with the best Spanish produce – in his bustling kitchens. I've provided sweet and savoury versions (see pages 25 and 26). These are perfect for serving at long, lazy lunches alongside a glass of crisp dry white wine or, my favourite, a cool pint of Spanish lager.

Madrid has so much to offer and this is particularly true when it comes to food. Its traditional bakes are perfect for celebrations, but also for sharing regularly with family and friends.

# CHURROS / Serves 6

Tucked away in a small alleyway in Madrid is Chocolatería San Ginés, a well-known institution of the city. It has a beautiful marble interior and only sells *churros* and thick hot chocolate for dipping them into. The queue is constantly around the block, but it's well worth the wait for their delicate deep-fried treats. I was lucky enough to be invited into their kitchen so that I could have a go at making *churros* on an industrial scale; it wasn't easy but it was great fun! Below is a simple version to try at home using the same basic ingredients that are used in Madrid.

**PREP:** 10 minutes

**PROVE:** 1 hour

**FRY:** 10 minutes

500ml water

1 teaspoon salt

350g plain flour

vegetable or sunflower oil,
   for deep frying

caster sugar or sugar
   mixed with ground
   cinnamon, for dusting

**equipment:**

piping bag fitted with
   a large star nozzle

1.  Place the water and salt in a pan and bring to the boil.

2.  Place the flour in a mixing bowl and make a well in the centre. Pour the boiling water into the well and whisk to combine with the flour, making sure you get rid of any lumps. This can also be done in a standing mixer. The batter should be smooth and firm. Let it stand for an hour.

3.  To cook the churros, heat the oil in a wide-based pan and test whether it's hot enough by dropping a piece of bread in. It should sizzle when it touches the oil.

4.  Put the batter into a piping bag fitted with a large star nozzle. Pipe 10cm strips of batter on to the surface of the oil and use scissors to snip them off. Fry the *churros* until golden brown, then drain on kitchen paper and sprinkle with the caster sugar or cinnamon sugar.

5.  Enjoy dunking into thick hot chocolate (see page 18).

# SPANISH HOT CHOCOLATE /

Serves 6

Hot chocolate and *churros* are still taken for breakfast in Madrid. Thicker than hot chocolate in the UK, the Spanish version is designed to coat the deep-fried *churros* strips. You will only need small cupfuls as it's very rich and filling.

**PREP:** 15 minutes

25g cocoa powder

25g caster sugar

25g cornflour

½ teaspoon ground cinnamon

500ml full-fat milk

40g dark chocolate, finely chopped or grated

1. Mix the cocoa powder, sugar, cornflour and cinnamon together in a bowl.

2. In a pan, gently heat the milk with the chopped chocolate until the chocolate has melted and the milk begins to simmer.

3. Pour the hot milk over the cocoa mixture and stir. Return to the pan, stirring all the time until the hot chocolate has thickened and is smooth. If it thickens too much, stir in some more cold milk.

4. Divide into small cups and enjoy with *churros* (see page 17).

# CHOCOLATE-DIPPED PALMIERS / Makes 14–16

These palm tree, or elephant ear, shaped pastries are, in fact, French. However, they were in every pastry shop in Madrid. The difference between these and their French counterparts is that the Spanish ones are made with lard from Ibérico pigs. Often served plain, but for a more indulgent treat, dip them in dark chocolate.

**PREP:** 20 minutes

**REST:** 1 hour

**BAKE:** 10 minutes

260g plain flour, plus extra for dusting

1 teaspoon salt

1 tablespoon caster sugar

185ml water

95g unsalted butter, frozen then grated

95g lard, frozen then grated

30g granulated sugar

150g dark chocolate, melted

1. To make the pastry, mix the flour, salt and caster sugar together in a bowl. Gradually add enough water to form a dough. Roll the dough out on a lightly floured work surface into a rectangle about 20cm x 30cm.

2. Scatter half the grated frozen butter and lard over the pastry. Fold down the top third of the pastry and fold up the bottom third, as if folding a letter.

3. Turn the folded dough through 90 degrees and roll it out into a rectangle again. Repeat the process, adding the remaining frozen butter and lard and folding as before. Roll out and repeat two more turns with the dough to create the layers in the pastry. Wrap the dough in clingfilm and leave to rest in the fridge for 30 minutes before using.

4. Sprinkle half the granulated sugar on the work surface. Roll the pastry out on top of the sugar to 30cm x 50cm. Scatter more sugar on top.

5. Starting from the long edge furthest away from you, roll the pastry tightly to the centre. Repeat from the other side so they meet in the middle. Wrap in clingfilm and place in the fridge for at least 30 minutes.

6. Preheat your oven to 200°C/Gas 6.

7. Cut slices 1.5cm thick and place on two baking trays lined with parchment paper. Bake for 10 minutes, then turn with a palette knife and cook the other side until crisp and golden. Cool on a wire rack, then dip in the melted chocolate. Place the palmiers on parchment paper and leave to set.

# IBÉRICO HAM AND MANCHEGO EMPANADA / Serves 4

Exploring the food in Madrid was fascinating and seeing how the *empanada* pastry was made was one of the highlights. The fat from the Ibérico pigs is used and this gives an amazing flavour and very crisp texture to the pastry. It feels silky and smooth as you eat it.

Here is my version, which you can try at home. The supreme Ibérico fat is hard to get hold of, so this pastry combines lard and butter. The filling is packed with my favourite ingredients I found out there: Ibérico ham, manchego cheese and roasted peppers.

**PREP:** 20 minutes

**REST:** 30 minutes

**BAKE:** 30–35 minutes

**for the pastry:**

175g plain flour, plus extra for dusting

½ teaspoon salt

125ml water

65g unsalted butter, frozen then grated, plus extra for greasing

65g lard, frozen then grated

**for the filling:**

a handful of spinach, leaves washed and stalks removed

100g roasted piquillo peppers from a jar, roughly chopped

100g manchego cheese, grated

50g Ibérico ham

1 beaten egg, to glaze

1. To make the pastry, mix the flour and salt together in a bowl. Gradually add enough water to form a dough – you may not need all the water.

2. Roll the dough out on a lightly floured work surface into a rectangle about 20cm x 30cm.

3. Scatter half the grated frozen butter and lard over the pastry. Fold down the top third and fold up the bottom third as if folding a letter.

4. Turn the folded dough through 90 degrees and roll it out into a rectangle again. Repeat the process, adding the remaining frozen butter and lard and folding as before. Working quickly, roll out and repeat two more turns with the dough to create the layers in the pastry. Wrap the dough in clingfilm and leave to rest in the fridge for 30 minutes before using.

5. Preheat your oven to 200°C/Gas 6.

6. Take the chilled pastry from the fridge and roll out on a lightly floured surface into a rectangle about 25cm x 35cm. Take the spinach and place on the base of half the pastry, leaving a 1.5cm gap from the edge. Next add the chopped peppers, cover with the grated cheese and top with the Ibérico ham. Brush the edge of the pastry with beaten egg. Fold the pastry in half to cover the filling and press the edges to seal. Brush the top with the beaten egg and score a pattern into the pastry with a knife, without cutting through it.

7. Place on a greased baking tray and bake for 30 to 35 minutes until the pastry is crisp and a rich golden brown colour. Leave to cool on the tray for 5 minutes, then cut into portions. Eat warm or cold with a salad.

# ORANGE AND ALMOND EMPANADA / Serves 4

This *empanada* is made as a rectangular bake, which is cut afterwards into portions. It is a traditional style and how a home cook might make it in Spain. The recipe combines the flavours of almond and orange, which were present in many of the sweet treats I tried whilst in Madrid. If you can find Spanish orange blossom water, it gives a really authentic flavour.

**PREP:** 20 minutes

**REST:** 30 minutes

**BAKE:** 30–35 minutes

### for the pastry:

175g plain flour, plus extra for dusting

½ teaspoon salt

125ml water

65g unsalted butter, frozen then grated, plus extra for greasing

65g lard, frozen then grated

### for the filling:

70g softened unsalted butter

70g caster sugar

2 medium eggs

35g plain flour

50g ground almonds

½ teaspoon orange blossom water

zest of 1 orange

1 beaten egg, to glaze

icing sugar, to dust

1. To make the pastry, mix the flour and salt together in a bowl. Gradually add enough water to form a dough – you may not need all the water.

2. Roll the dough out on a lightly floured work surface into a rectangle about 20cm x 30cm.

3. Scatter half of the grated frozen butter and lard over the pastry. Fold down the top third and fold up the bottom third, as if folding a letter.

4. Turn the folded dough through 90 degrees and roll it out into a rectangle again. Repeat the process, adding the remaining frozen butter and lard and folding as before. Working quickly, roll out and repeat two more turns with the dough – this will create the layers in the pastry. Wrap the dough in clingfilm and leave to rest in the fridge for 30 minutes before using.

5. Preheat your oven to 200°C/Gas 6.

6. To make the filling, beat the butter and caster sugar until all the sugar has dissolved and the mixture is pale and fluffy. Add the eggs one at a time and mix. Add the flour and ground almonds and stir to form a thick paste. Add the orange blossom water and orange zest, mix well and set to one side.

7. Take the chilled pastry from the fridge and roll out on a lightly floured surface into a rectangle about 25cm x 35cm. Spread the filling over half the pastry, leaving a 1.5cm gap from the edge. Brush the edge of the pastry with the beaten egg. Fold the pastry in half to cover the filling. Press the edges to seal. Brush the top with beaten egg and score a pattern on the top with a knife, without cutting through the pastry.

8. Place on a greased baking tray and bake for 30 to 35 minutes until the pastry is crisp and a rich golden brown colour. Leave to cool on the tray for 5 minutes, cut into portions and dust with icing sugar. This is delicious served either warm or cold.

# ROSCÓN DE REYES / Makes 1 large ring

The 'Ring of Kings' is a celebratory cake in Spain. Originally made to celebrate the gifts the three kings brought to Jesus, it is traditionally eaten on January 6th. Popular in Madrid, and then adopted by the nobility of Europe, the cake usually contains a hidden surprise inside, such as coins. This custom spread to all classes of society, with the coins being substituted with tiny figurines made out of beans. It was believed that whoever got the slice containing these would have good luck for the coming year. My recipe doesn't include any hidden surprises, but if you do want to include any then stir them into the mixture when adding the cake dough to the bread dough, and make sure you warn your guests before they tuck in! The unusual combination of a yeasted dough mixed with a sponge gives a lovely light texture to the cake.

**PREP:** 30 minutes

**PROVE:** 2–4 hours

**BAKE:** 30–35 minutes

**for the dough:**

250g strong white bread flour, plus extra for dusting

7g instant yeast

½ teaspoon salt

zest of 1 orange

120–140ml water

**for the cake:**

170g caster sugar

170g softened unsalted butter

3 medium eggs

2 egg yolks

250g self-raising flour

2 tablespoons full-fat milk

zest of 1 orange

2–3 tablespoons orange extract or orange blossom water

1 beaten egg, to glaze

50g chopped almonds

30g caster sugar

1. Begin by making the yeast dough. Place the strong flour in a bowl, add the yeast to one side and the salt to the other. Add the orange zest, then gradually add the water and use your hand to bring the dough together. The dough will be rough at this stage. Tip on to a lightly floured surface and knead until you have a smooth, stiff dough. This will take 5 to 10 minutes. Cover and leave to double in size – this will take about an hour.

2. For the cake mix, beat the sugar and butter together until light and fluffy. Add the eggs and yolks and beat again. Fold in the flour and mix until combined. Add the milk, orange zest and extract and mix well.

3. Take the risen dough and place in the bowl of a mixer fitted with a dough hook. On a slow speed, gradually add spoonfuls of the cake mix until it is all incorporated. Increase the speed and mix for 8 to 10 minutes until you have a sticky dough. Cover with clingfilm and leave to prove until doubled in size – this can take between 1 to 3 hours.

4. Line a large baking tray with parchment paper.

5. Tip the dough on to a heavily floured work surface. It will be soft and tricky to handle. Form into a cylinder and join the ends together to form a large circle. Place on the prepared tray, put the tray into a clean plastic bag and leave to prove for 1 hour or until risen.

6. Preheat your oven to 200°C/Gas 6. Remove the tray from the plastic bag and brush the ring with the egg wash. Sprinkle the top with alternate patches of chopped almonds and sugar. Bake for 20 minutes, then reduce the heat to 180°C/Gas 4 and bake for 10 to 15 minutes. The ring should be golden brown and cooked through. Cool on a wire rack.

# SPANISH SABLE BISCUITS /

Makes 25–30

I tried these biscuits in Madrid, at a bakery and café called El Riojano. They came with a selection of other types of biscuits to accompany my coffee and, although they were the plainest and simplest on the plate, they were definitely my favourite. I love the egg glaze pattern on them. If you are in Madrid, do make sure to pop into El Riojano, located at Calle Mayor, 10 – it's a spectacular shop with a tea room at the back. It has been there since 1855 and was started by Queen Isabel's confectioner; it certainly feels like you've stepped back in time. All the products are very high quality and you will be spoilt for choice. This recipe is my tribute to them.

**PREP:** 15 minutes

**REST:** 1 hour

**BAKE:** 12–14 minutes

230g plain flour, plus extra for dusting

150g firm unsalted butter, cut into small pieces

115g icing sugar, sifted

a pinch of salt

3 large egg yolks

½ teaspoon vanilla extract

2–3 teaspoons cold water

2 egg yolks beaten together with 1 tablespoon caster sugar, to glaze

**equipment:**

7cm fluted cutter

1. Place the flour, butter, icing sugar and salt in a mixing bowl. Rub together until it resembles breadcrumbs. Add the egg yolks and vanilla extract and mix well. Add the water, a teaspoon at a time, and bring the mixture together; you may not need all the water.

2. On a lightly floured surface, knead gently to form a smooth ball of dough. Wrap in clingfilm and place in the fridge for at least 30 minutes.

3. Line two trays with parchment paper.

4. On a lightly floured surface, roll out the dough to 5mm thick. Using a 7cm fluted cutter, stamp out 25 to 30 rounds. You will need to re-roll the trimmings. Place the biscuits on to the prepared trays, brush with some of the egg yolk glaze, and place in the fridge to rest for 30 minutes.

5. Preheat your oven to 180°C/Gas 4.

6. Just before baking, brush with the egg glaze again. Use a fork and press gently to draw wavy lines through the egg wash and the surface of the biscuit. Bake for 12 to 14 minutes until golden brown and shiny. The biscuits will be soft whilst warm, so leave on the tray for a few minutes until they have set, then transfer to a wire rack to cool.

# BUÑUELOS DE VIENTO / Serves 6

My good friend and chef Omar Allibhoy, owner of Tapas Revolution in London, took me on a gastronomic guide of his home city of Madrid. We visited the oldest patisserie, called El Riojano, where I tried lots of pastries and biscuits. I particularly enjoyed the *buñuelos de viento*, which translates to 'puffs of wind'. They are very light pastry puffs, or dough balls, made to celebrate All Saints' Day in Spain, and are often filled with milk, cream or chocolate. Omar has kindly shared his recipe for them below.

**PREP:** 15 minutes

**FRY:** 5 minutes

100ml water

45g unsalted butter

2g table salt

75g plain flour

3 medium eggs

vegetable oil, for frying

caster or icing sugar,
  for dusting

optional: whipped cream

1. Place the water, butter and salt in a pan and bring to the boil. Add the flour and mix with a wooden spoon for about 1 minute until well combined. The mixture should become a ball that separates from the walls of the pan. Remove from the heat.

2. Add the eggs, one at a time, mixing each one into the dough using a wooden spoon until completely integrated before adding the next. The mixture should have the consistency of thick yoghurt.

3. Pour enough oil into a deep pan to give you two fingers' depth of it. Heat until a cube of day-old bread dropped in the oil turns golden in about 30 seconds. Alternatively, heat a deep-fat fryer to 180°C.

4. Use a couple of spoons to shape pieces of the dough into rounds the size of a walnut. Drop them carefully into the hot oil. The dough should start frying and puff up immediately; after a few seconds they will turn over by themselves. Leave them in the oil for about 5 minutes until they turn golden brown. Scoop out with a slotted spoon and drain on kitchen paper. They should have a delicate crispness on the outside and be pretty much all air on the inside.

5. Dust with caster or icing sugar whilst still warm. If you want to fill with whipped cream, make a little cut on the side of each of them and use a piping bag to fill.

6. You could also try filling these with chocolate ganache (see page 188) or crème pâtissière (see page 87).

# SQUID INK AND SWEET PEPPER BREAD / Makes 1 loaf

Fourth-generation baker Paco Fernandez from Viena la Baguette showed me round his artisan bakery in Madrid. Unlike other European countries, the Spanish don't have a strong bread culture – it's not valued in the same way as their olives, wines and ham. However, Paco is trying to buck this trend by creating some interesting breads and unique flavour combinations. His black bread flavoured with squid ink and dried peppers was pretty special. Very striking visually, with a subtle salty sea flavour from the squid ink, which is balanced by the sweet peppers. He didn't pass on the recipe to me (trade secret!) so I have developed my own version. I couldn't find the dried pimento flakes available in Spain, so I used dried sweet peppers from a deli and chopped them finely.

**PREP:** 15 minutes

**PROVE:** 9–13 hours

**BAKE:** 30–35 minutes

500g strong white bread flour, plus extra for dusting

8g salt

3g instant yeast

16g squid ink (4 small sachets)

1 teaspoon black food colouring powder

3 dried peppers, stalks removed and finely chopped

2 tablespoons olive oil, plus extra for oiling

300–320ml cool water

**equipment:**

it's a good idea to use a mixer with a dough hook to avoid getting black food colouring everywhere

1. Place the flour in the bowl of a mixer fitted with a dough hook. Place the salt at one side and the yeast at the other. Add the squid ink, black food colouring powder, dried peppers and olive oil.

2. Begin mixing on a slow speed and add three quarters of the water. As the dough starts to come together, slowly add the remaining water. Mix for 5 to 8 minutes on a medium setting until the dough is smooth and stretchy. Place in a lightly oiled bowl, cover and put into the fridge for 8 to 12 hours to prove slowly.

3. Remove the dough from the bowl and place on a lightly floured surface. Knock the air out of the dough by repeatedly folding it in on itself. Once smooth, form the dough into a round cob shape. Place on a baking tray, cover with a clean plastic bag and leave to prove for at least an hour or until doubled in size. It should spring back if you prod it lightly with your finger.

4. Preheat the oven to 220°C/Gas 7. Place a roasting tin in the bottom of the oven to heat up.

5. When ready to bake, dust the bread with flour, then slash it twice deeply with a knife. Fill the hot roasting tray with hot water – this will create steam and help form a crust on the bread. Place the baking tray on a shelf above the water and bake the bread for 30 to 35 minutes until it is cooked through and sounds hollow when tapped on the base. Cool on a wire rack.

# TORTA / Makes 3

A rustic Spanish classic. When I tasted this flatbread made with 70 per cent olive oil, I was absolutely blown away. Paco Fernandez from Viena la Baguette bakery developed it to eat alongside the famous Ibérico ham and it has a rich, fruity flavour from the oil. I decided to use a little less in my recipe, but it still has lots of flavour. I would suggest you only make this if you have a mixer with a dough hook, as it takes time for the mixture to incorporate the oil and form into a dough.

**PREP:** 15 minutes

**PROVE:** 9–13 hours

**BAKE:** 15–20 minutes

500g strong white bread flour, plus extra for dusting

8g salt

5g instant yeast

225ml extra virgin olive oil, plus extra for oiling

120ml water

20g flaky sea salt

1. Place the flour in the bowl of a mixer fitted with a dough hook. Place the salt at one side and the yeast at the other. Add the olive oil and begin mixing on a slow speed. Slowly add the water until the mixture forms a soft dough. Mix for 5 to 8 minutes on a medium setting until the dough is smooth. Place in a lightly oiled bowl, cover and put into the fridge for 8 to 12 hours to prove slowly.

2. Line three baking trays with parchment paper. Remove the dough from the bowl and place on a lightly floured surface. Knock the air out of the dough by repeatedly folding it in on itself. Divide into three equal pieces and roll each one into a circle (about 20cm in diameter). Place one torta on each tray and place the trays inside clean plastic bags. Leave to prove for an hour or until doubled in size.

3. Preheat your oven to 220°C/Gas 7. Brush the surface of the dough with olive oil and sprinkle the top with a little sea salt. Make indentations by pushing your fingers into the dough until you touch the tray.

4. Bake for 15 to 20 minutes or until risen and golden brown.

# LA DOLCE VITA /

## NAPLES

Rum babas / Pizza Margherita / Chocolate pizza /
Caprese cake / Casatiello / Gattò di Santa Chiara /
Garlic ciabatta / Focaccia / Pizza pie

Naples is a loud, ancient metropolis with an abundance of museums, galleries, castles and other amazing archaeological sites, not to mention a bustling business district. But the real fun to be had in this city is down its side streets. Put your map aside and see where the lanes and alleys take you – it's the best way to discover all the incredible food this city has to offer.

For many people, Neapolitan food means pizza Margherita. There is so much more to the cuisine here, but I couldn't visit without trying one for myself and there's no better place than Antica Pizzeria Port'Alba. Established in 1738 and nestled away amongst some really charming bookshops, this is widely believed to be the world's oldest pizzeria. It's well worth a visit, particularly given its rich history. Another connoisseur of this dish is maverick chef Enzo Coccia, who owns two restaurants in the city. One of Enzo's restaurants serves traditional pizza and the other, gourmet pizza – needless to say, the latter causes quite some contention amongst the locals. For a fail-safe version, see my recipe on page 50.

Neapolitans are, in my experience, very passionate about their food, and chefs Raffaele and Salvatore Capparelli are no exception. I had the pleasure of visiting them in their respective *pasticcerie*, Patisserie Capparelli and Pasticceria Capriccio, both of which serve exceptional pastries. Naples born and bred, Raffaele and Salvatore showed me a giant version of the classic *babà al rum,* a rich cake soaked in liquor and often filled with whipped cream or custard. See page 49 for my recipe. They're perfect with a good espresso. If you've a sweet tooth, I'd also highly recommend going to Scaturchio, supposedly Naples' oldest *pasticceria*, which is set on one of its prettiest piazzas. Make sure to try their *sfogliatella*, a shell-shaped pastry, and (if you have room) their *ministeriale*, a rich, dark chocolate cake filled with rum-infused cream.

Speaking of passionate – I am so pleased that I had the chance to spend time with my old friend Gennaro Contaldo on my Neapolitan break. He's worked with so many brilliant chefs and his passion for Amalfitan cuisine is clear. Who better to enjoy a nice cool glass of limoncello with? His recipe for a Neapolitan bread called *casatiello* is on page 58 and it's perfect to share with friends and family.

Neapolitans are passionate about their city and with good reason. Rich in cultural and culinary history, there is so much to enjoy here and there's always something happening. Simply roam around, find a piazza or *pasticceria* and sit outside with a pastry and a coffee, taking it all in.

# RUM BABAS / Makes 8

A Neapolitan classic, individual rum babas are little yeast cakes that are soaked in rum before serving, giving them an alcoholic kick. Sometimes they are filled with whipped cream or custard. Whichever way, they are sticky, sweet and delicious; try them with a strong espresso.

**PREP:** 10 minutes

**PROVE:** 1–3 hours

**BAKE:** 10–12 minutes

### for the dough:

250g strong white bread flour

70g softened unsalted butter, plus extra for greasing

3g salt

30g caster sugar

5g instant yeast

3 medium eggs

1 teaspoon vanilla extract

### for the syrup:

150g caster sugar

250ml water

200ml rum

### equipment:

8 dariole moulds (6.5cm x 6cm)

1. To make the dough, place the flour in the bowl of a mixer fitted with a dough hook. Add the butter, salt and sugar to one side of the bowl and the yeast to the other side. On a slow speed begin to mix, adding the eggs one at a time, then the vanilla extract, and mixing until all the ingredients are incorporated. Increase the speed and mix for 5 minutes until the dough is thoroughly combined. The mix will be very sticky at this stage. Cover and leave to prove until the dough has doubled in size. This will take between 1 and 3 hours.

2. Grease eight dariole moulds (6.5cm x 6cm) with butter. Once proved, scoop out handfuls of dough. Gently swing the dough to stretch it, then place in the moulds so they are half full. Leave to prove until the mixture rises 1cm above the moulds.

3. For the syrup, heat the sugar and water to dissolve the sugar, but do not boil. Add the rum and stir to combine. Turn off the heat and leave to cool.

4. Preheat your oven to 200°C/Gas 6. Bake the babas for 10 to 12 minutes until risen and golden brown. Leave to cool for a few minutes before removing from the moulds.

5. One at a time, place the babas in the syrup, turning so they are soaked all the way through. Transfer to a plate. Serve with the remaining rum syrup.

# PIZZA MARGHERITA / Serves 4

Enzo Coccia from Naples is an encyclopaedia of pizza knowledge. He has perfected the art of pizza making and turned it into a science. Like all top chefs, he controls every aspect of the process: the quality of the ingredients – from the flour and water to the toppings – the humidity when proving and the oven temperature are all key to the end result. Enzo only cooks his pizzas for 45 seconds because his wood-burning oven reaches 465°C! Without a wood burner, it is difficult to replicate his pizzas at home, but here are a few tips I picked up that will improve your pizza making:

- Leave the dough to prove for 10 hours. This helps develop the flavour of the crust.

- Don't put too much sauce and topping on the pizza as it will make the base soggy and it won't cook through.

- Use the very best ingredients you can find. Enzo uses the local San Marzano tomatoes, which are sweet. If you're lucky enough to live near an Italian deli, you may be able to get them in tins, otherwise use tinned cherry tomatoes as they are less acidic.

- Use a combination of mozzarella and fresh Parmesan; the creamy mozzarella is balanced with the salty Parmesan.

- Always drizzle your pizza with a little olive oil before baking.

**PREP:** 30 minutes

**PROVE:** 10–12 hours

**BAKE:** 8–10 minutes
  per pizza

**for the pizza dough:**

300g strong white bread flour,
  plus extra for dusting

1 teaspoon salt

½ teaspoon instant yeast

180ml cold water

olive oil, for greasing

**for the tomato sauce:**

1 x 400g tin of cherry
  tomatoes

1 clove of garlic, crushed

½ teaspoon sugar

1 tablespoon olive oil

salt and freshly ground
  black pepper

**for the topping:**

buffalo mozzarella

grated Parmesan cheese

olive oil, for drizzling

fresh basil leaves, to serve

**equipment:**

silicone baking mat
  (if you don't have silicone,
  a heavily floured baking
  sheet will also work)
  and a pizza stone or flat
  baking tray

1. To make the pizza dough, place the flour in a bowl and add the salt to one side and the yeast to the other. Gradually add the water and mix to form a soft dough. You may not need to use all the water.

2. Turn the dough out on to an oiled work surface and knead for 5 to 10 minutes, or until the dough is smooth and elastic. Cut off a small piece of the dough and stretch part of it as thinly as you can. If you can see the shadow of your fingers through the dough (the light should shine through the dough like a windowpane) without tearing, it is ready to prove. Shape the dough into a ball, place in a bowl, cover and leave to rest for 15 minutes.

3. Make the tomato sauce by tipping the tin of tomatoes into a frying pan. On a medium to high heat, cook until the liquid has evaporated. Squash the cherry tomatoes with a wooden spoon and stir until you have a thick sauce. Turn off the heat and stir in the remaining sauce ingredients. Leave to cool.

4. Divide the dough into four balls, cover loosely and leave somewhere cool for 10–12 hours.

5. Stretch or roll the dough into thin 22cm circles. Place a circle on a piece of silicone so the pizza can be easily transferred to the oven later. If you don't have silicone, a heavily floured baking sheet will also work.

6. Place a pizza stone or flat baking tray on the top shelf in your oven and heat to 220°C/Gas 7. If your oven has a fan setting with grill, then use this but keep your eye on the pizza to avoid it burning. Place the pizza dough on the hot tray and bake for 2 minutes. This will start to cook the pizza.

7. Remove the part-cooked pizza base from the oven and spread a little of the tomato sauce over the base. Add chunks of the mozzarella cheese and sprinkle with Parmesan. Drizzle over a little olive oil. Return the pizza back to the oven and bake for 6 to 8 minutes, or until the base is golden brown and the topping is bubbling. Repeat with the remaining pizzas. Sprinkle with fresh basil leaves just before serving.

# CHOCOLATE PIZZA / Makes 4

For dessert at his restaurant La Notizia in Naples, Enzo Coccia served chocolate pizza, which went down extremely well with all the children eating there. The dough should be slightly thicker than a normal pizza base before cooking as you need to slice it horizontally to put the filling in. It's the same dough recipe as for the savoury pizza on page 51 so you could leave it for the 10-hour prove, but I don't think the kids will notice if they can't wait that long!

**PREP:** 20 minutes

**PROVE:** 45 minutes

**BAKE:** 7–9 minutes per pizza

### for the pizza dough:

300g strong white bread flour, plus extra for dusting

1 teaspoon salt

½ teaspoon instant yeast

180ml cold water

olive oil, for greasing

### for the filling:

200g chocolate spread

### equipment:

silicone baking mat (if you don't have silicone, a heavily floured baking sheet will also work) and a pizza stone or flat baking tray

1. To make the pizza dough, place the flour in a bowl and add the salt to one side and the yeast to the other. Gradually add the water and mix to form a soft dough. You may not need to use all the water.

2. Turn the dough out on to an oiled work surface and knead for 5 to 10 minutes, or until the dough is smooth and elastic. Cut off a small piece of the dough and stretch part of it as thinly as you can. If you can see the shadow of your fingers through the dough (the light should shine through the dough like a windowpane) without it tearing, it is ready to prove. Shape the dough into a ball, place in a bowl, cover and leave to rest for 45 minutes.

3. Stretch or roll the dough into four pitta shapes. Make sure they're not too thin as you need to slice them once cooked, but also not too thick as you want them to puff up and cook through. Place one base on a piece of silicone so it can be easily transferred to the oven later.

4. Place a pizza stone or flat baking tray on the top shelf of your oven and heat the oven to 220°C/Gas 7. Place the dough base on the hot tray and bake for 7 to 9 minutes. The base should be cooked through, risen and just beginning to colour. Repeat with the remaining pizzas.

5. Once each pizza is cooked, put it on to a chopping board and insert a knife into the side. Carefully slice the pizza, but not all the way through, so you can flip open the top. Whilst the base is still warm, spread with chocolate spread, then close the lid back down and cut into pieces. Serve straight away.

# CAPRESE CAKE / Serves 8–10

When I visited the stunning Amalfi coast in Italy I was lucky enough to spend some time with Andrea Pansa, a fifth-generation baker. His Pasticceria Pansa in Amalfi is a treasure trove of sweet delights. When his recipes, like this Caprese cake, call for ground almonds, Andrea never uses pre-ground almonds; instead he grinds them himself with a little sugar as this gives a better flavour. Amalfi is famous for its lemon groves and Andrea grows his own, which he uses in many of his products. His candied peel was definitely some of the finest I've ever tasted. Whilst it's not a traditional garnish, I couldn't resist using some to decorate this cake, which comes from the beautiful island of Capri.

**PREP:** 20 minutes

**BAKE:** 40–45 minutes

**for the cake:**

unsalted butter, for greasing

100g whole almonds

210g caster sugar

1 whole medium egg

5 medium eggs, separated

265g dark chocolate, melted

50g chopped almonds

**for the topping:**

70ml water

90g caster sugar

30g cocoa powder

25ml liquid glucose

2 gelatine sheets (approx. 2.4g)

candied lemon or chopped almonds, to decorate

**equipment:**

20cm deep round tin

1. Preheat your oven to 180°C/Gas 4. Grease a 20cm deep round tin.

2. To make the cake, begin by grinding the whole almonds with 50g of the sugar in a food processor.

3. Beat the whole egg, the 5 egg yolks and the remaining 160g of caster sugar until the mix is pale and creamy and leaves a trail on the surface.

4. Whisk the egg whites to soft peaks.

5. Mix the cooled, melted chocolate with the egg yolk and sugar mixture. Stir in the ground almonds and chopped the almonds. Beat in a spoonful of egg whites to loosen the mixture. Now gently fold in the remaining egg whites, a spoonful at a time. Pour the mixture into the prepared tin and bake for 40 to 45 minutes.

6. To prepare the topping, place the water, sugar, cocoa powder and glucose in a saucepan and bring to the boil. Simmer for 5 minutes and stir. Soften the gelatine in a little water. Remove the pan from the heat. Squeeze any liquid from the gelatine and add the sheets to the pan. Stir until they have dissolved. Leave to cool.

7. Once the cake is cooked, leave in the tin to cool before turning out on to a serving plate.

8. Pour the chocolate topping just on the top surface of the cake and decorate with the candied lemon or extra chopped almonds.

# CASATIELLO / Makes 1 large ring

I had such a great time being shown round Naples by my friend, Gennaro Contaldo. He has very kindly allowed me to include his recipe for his favourite type of Neapolitan bread which he loves to make at Easter. He advises that the eggs should be used at room temperature; too cold and they willl stop the dough from rising. This is a great recipe for using up any leftover ham, salami or cheese.

**PREP:** 25 minutes

**PROVE:** 40 minutes

**BAKE:** 30 minutes

100g salami, cut into
  small cubes

100g pancetta, cut into
  small cubes

100g prosciutto, cut into
  small cubes

100g provolone cheese,
  cut into small cubes

100g pecorino cheese,
  cut into small cubes

100g Parmesan cheese,
  grated

2 tablespoons black pepper

25g fresh yeast

450ml lukewarm water

600g strong white bread flour,
  plus extra for dusting

1 teaspoon salt

semolina flour or
  breadcrumbs, to sprinkle

optional: 6 eggs

1. Place the cured meats and cheeses in a bowl with the black pepper, mix well and set aside.

2. Dissolve the yeast in the lukewarm water. Combine the bread flour and salt, add the yeast mixture and mix with your hands, gradually incorporating all the bread flour until you have a soft, sticky dough. Turn out on to a floured work surface and knead for about 3 minutes or until smooth, adding more flour to the surface if necessary. Break off a piece of dough, roughly the size of a tennis ball, and set aside. Spread the remaining dough into a roughly round shape and add the meat and cheese mixture, kneading it into the dough until evenly combined. Continue to knead for a couple of minutes, then roll the dough into a large sausage shape about 65cm long and seal the ends to form a ring.

3. Sprinkle some semolina flour or breadcrumbs on to a baking tray and place the ring on top. If using the eggs, make six deep incisions with a sharp knife around the top of the ring at roughly equal spaces and with your fingers, enlarge each one to make a pocket. Place an egg lying flat in each pocket.

4. Take the remaining piece of dough, roll out into a rough square and cut out 12 strips approximately 7.5cm long. Place two strips crisscross over each egg, brushing with a little water so they stick well. Cover the bread with a cloth and leave in a warm place to rest for about 40 minutes until it has doubled in size.

5. Meanwhile, preheat the oven to 220°C/Gas 7.

6. Bake the bread for 30 minutes or until golden. Delicious served hot or cold.

# GATTÒ DI SANTA CHIARA /

Serves 8–10

This is a recipe from the Campania region of Italy and it's like a cross between a quiche and a savoury cake. Sometimes it's the simple recipes that are the best, and this definitely applies here. Bread dough mixed with potato and packed with ham, cheese and herbs gives a light and airy cake full of flavour. Good enough to eat on its own or the perfect accompaniment to pasta dishes and salads.

**PREP:** 30 minutes

**PROVE:** 1 hour

**BAKE:** 35–40 minutes

125g (about 1 small) potato

250g strong white bread flour,
  plus extra for dusting

7g instant yeast

1 teaspoon salt

125ml water

50g lard, plus extra
  for greasing

1–2 medium eggs

125g mozzarella,
  cut into small cubes

100g Parma ham,
  cut into strips

2 sprigs of fresh rosemary,
  cut into small sprigs

olive oil

sea salt

**equipment:**

25cm loose bottom cake tin

potato ricer

1. Boil the potato in its skin until cooked through.

2. Place 200g of the flour in a bowl with the yeast on one side and the salt on the other. Slowly add half the water and mix the ingredients together to form a soft dough. Add more water if required. Knead on a floured surface until smooth. Place in a bowl, cover and leave to rise for about an hour or until doubled in size.

3. Grease a 25cm loose bottom cake tin with lard. Use the remaining 50g of flour to dust your work surface again. Tip the dough on to the flour and knock back. Take the potato, remove the skin and then, using a potato ricer, rice the potato on to the dough. Add the 50g of lard and 1 egg. Fold the dough on to itself many times to incorporate the ingredients. If the dough is too dry, add the other egg. Knead for 10 minutes until you have a smooth, silky dough.

4. Shape the dough into a rectangle and top with the mozzarella and ham. Fold the dough in on itself again so the cheese and ham are evenly distributed throughout.

5. Shape the dough into a ball and place in the prepared tin, pressing down so it fits the edges of the tin. Cover and leave to prove for about an hour. Preheat your oven to 190°C/Gas 5.

6. Just before baking, push sprigs of rosemary deep into the surface of the dough. Brush with a little olive oil and sprinkle with a little sea salt. Bake for 35 to 40 minutes until golden. Leave to cool in the tin for 5 to 10 minutes before removing.

# GARLIC CIABATTA / Makes 2 loaves

With its characteristic open texture, ciabatta is a great bread for sharing. In this recipe I have slowly cooked the garlic cloves in olive oil to give a subtly sweet flavour throughout the bread. It's a straightforward one to make and such a great accompaniment to any pasta dish.

**PREP:** 50 minutes–1 hour

**PROVE:** 1–2 hours

**BAKE:** 25 minutes

150ml olive oil, plus extra for oiling

1 bulb of garlic, cloves separated and peeled

500g strong white bread flour, plus extra for dusting

10g salt

10g instant yeast

350–370ml cool water

optional: semolina, for dusting

**equipment:**

2–3 litre square plastic container

1. Lightly oil a 2–3 litre square plastic container. Using a square tub will help to shape the dough.

2. Put the oil and the garlic cloves into a small saucepan and gently simmer for about 15 to 20 minutes until soft but not coloured. Remove the garlic and set aside to cool. Pour the oil into a measuring jug and leave to cool.

3. Put the flour, salt and yeast into the bowl of a mixer fitted with a dough hook, keeping the salt and yeast separate. Add 50ml of the cooled olive oil and three quarters of the water and begin mixing on a slow speed. As the dough comes together, gradually add the rest of the water. Mix for a further 5 to 8 minutes until the dough is smooth and stretchy. It will be wetter than a standard dough.

4. Add the garlic cloves and mix for another 5 minutes so that they break down and are distributed through the dough. Tip the dough mixture into the prepared tub and cover with cling-film, then leave until at least doubled or, even better, trebled in size – 1 to 2 hours or longer.

5. Preheat the oven to 220°C/Gas 7 and line two baking trays with parchment paper.

6. Dust your work surface heavily with flour and semolina too, if you have some. Carefully tip the dough (it will be very wet) on to the work surface, trying to keep a rough square shape. Instead of knocking it back, try to handle it gently so that you keep as much air in the dough as possible. Coat the top of the dough with more flour or semolina. Cut the dough in half lengthways so that you end up with two long strips of dough.

7. Carefully place the two strips of dough on the baking trays and leave to rest for a further 10 minutes. Bake for 15 minutes, then drop the oven temperature to 190°C/Gas 5 and bake for another 10 minutes or until cooked through. Tap the bottom of the loaves to check that they sound hollow, then cool on a wire rack.

# FOCACCIA / Makes 1 loaf

A big favourite of mine, and simple to make, is the Italian flatbread called focaccia. This one is flavoured with typical Italian ingredients: olives, tomatoes and basil. Don't be afraid to make it your own, though, by changing the flavours – cheese, onion and chargrilled peppers all work well.

**PREP:** 15 minutes

**PROVE:** 2–4 hours

**BAKE:** 20–25 minutes

500g strong white bread flour

10g salt

10g instant yeast

50ml olive oil, plus extra
for oiling

350ml cool water

30g black olives, roughly
chopped

50g sun-blush tomatoes,
roughly chopped

2 tablespoons finely chopped
fresh basil leaves

olive oil, to finish

flaky sea salt, to finish

**equipment:**

20cm x 34cm baking tray

1. Put the flour, salt and yeast into the bowl of a mixer fitted with a dough hook, keeping the salt on one side and the yeast on the other.

2. Add the olive oil and three-quarters of the water and begin mixing slowly. As the dough comes together, add the remaining water and continue to mix for about 5 minutes until you have a very soft dough – wetter than a standard bread dough. Tip this into an oiled bowl, cover and leave to rise for 1 to 3 hours until at least doubled in size.

3. Oil your work surface and tip the dough out. Gently knock it back into a large square shape and sprinkle the olives, tomatoes and basil over the surface. Fold the dough over to incorporate the ingredients and carefully knead so that they are distributed through the bread. Shape the dough into roughly the size of a 20cm x 34cm baking tray. Oil the tray and place the dough on it.

4. Put the tray into a clean plastic bag and leave to prove for about an hour or so until the dough is doubled in size and springs back quickly if you prod it with your finger.

5. Meanwhile, preheat your oven to 220°C/Gas 7.

6. Make deep dimples in the focaccia with your fingers, pushing all the way to the bottom of the dough. Drizzle with more olive oil and sprinkle with a little flaky sea salt. Bake for 10 minutes, then turn the oven down to 190°C/Gas 5 and bake for a further 10 to 15 minutes until it is golden brown and cooked through. Tap the bottom of the focaccia and it should sound hollow. Drizzle with a little more olive oil, then cool on a wire rack.

# PIZZA PIE / Serves 6

I was delighted when I discovered this recipe: two of my favourite dishes, pizza and pie, combined! Originally from the Campania region of Italy, this pie was eaten during the Christmas period. The main ingredient for the filling is a green called escarole, a member of the endive family but less bitter in flavour. Try to get hold of some if you can, otherwise you can use chicory and kale as I have done here. You can also use chard and spinach.

**PREP:** 35 minutes

**PROVE:** 1 hour

**BAKE:** 30–40 minutes

**for the pastry:**

350g strong white bread flour, plus extra for dusting

7g instant yeast

½ teaspoon salt

1 medium egg

75g softened unsalted butter, plus extra for greasing

125–150ml warm full-fat milk

olive oil, for greasing

**for the filling:**

2 heads of chicory

150g kale

50ml olive oil

3 cloves of garlic, crushed

5 salted anchovy fillets

75g pitted olives, rinsed and roughly chopped

30g capers, rinsed

a little salt and freshly ground black pepper

200g provolone cheese

10–12 fresh basil leaves, torn

1 beaten egg, to glaze

**equipment:**

20cm loose bottom tart tin

1. Place the flour in a large mixing bowl. Add the yeast to one side and the salt to the other. Add the egg, butter and three quarters of the warm milk. Use your hand to bring all the ingredients together. Gradually add the remaining milk to form the dough. Tip the dough on to a lightly floured surface and knead for 5 to 10 minutes until smooth. Place in a lightly oiled bowl, cover and leave to prove for about an hour.

2. To make the filling, bring a large pan of salted water to the boil. Wash and trim the chicory, then slice. Wash the kale, remove any stalks and tear into small pieces. Cook the chicory and kale in the water for 2 minutes. Drain thoroughly, then pat dry with kitchen paper.

3. In a wide sauté pan, heat the oil and add the garlic and anchovies. Over a medium heat, cook until the anchovies break down a bit and the garlic has softened. Use a slotted spoon and remove the garlic and anchovies from the pan. Cook the chicory and kale in the remaining oil over a high heat until all the moisture has evaporated. Add the olives and capers and stir to combine. Remove from the heat and return the anchovies and garlic to the pan. Give the filling a good stir and check the seasoning. Be careful with the salt as the anchovies and capers are salty. Add lots of black pepper. Leave to go cold, then fold in the grated cheese and torn basil leaves.

4. Preheat your oven to 180°C/Gas 4 and grease a 20cm loose bottom tart tin.

5. Tip the dough on to a lightly floured surface and cut off a third of the dough to use as a lid. Roll the big piece of dough into a large circle 5mm thick. Line the prepared tin with the dough and trim the edge to neaten. Tip the filling into the lined tin and press down to level the surface.

6. Roll the remaining pastry into a lid, brush the edge of the pastry in the tin with egg wash, then place the lid on top of the filling. It will sit just below the top of the tin. Fold down the sides of the pie on to the lid and pinch the edges together to seal. Roll out any offcuts to make decorations and stick on the lid with the egg wash. Make a small slit in the top of the pie to let any steam escape whilst cooking, then glaze with egg wash and bake for 30 to 40 minutes until the dough is cooked and golden brown.

7. Leave to cool in the tin for 15 minutes before removing. Eat warm or cold.

# FRENCH FANCIES /

## PARIS

Croissants / Quiche Lorraine / Éclairs / Madeleines / Fig and apricot tart /
Châtaigne / Brioche / French square jammy dodgers / Baguettes /
Pear and almond tart / Chocolate and hazelnut meringues

France: the land of bread and wine, of croissants and cheese. What a great place to visit if you love food and want to taste some of the world's very best produce. From London you can nip on the Eurostar to spend a few days in Paris or if, like me, you prefer to drive there, it's dead easy to use the Channel Tunnel crossing. I went with a firm idea of the addresses I wanted to visit and the bakers I wanted to meet.

Baking is held in such high regard in France that there are prizes awarded to those who are producing the very best types of breads. Interestingly, there are no big flashy signs heralding these bakers' status – instead just a subtle logo on the bakery window. There are more than 35,000 bakeries in France, so imagine how many baguettes and croissants are made every day! I headed straight to Arnaud Delmontel in the 9th arrondissement to try their baguettes, which were voted the best in the country in 2007. With such talented bakers across the entire length and breadth of France, this is a staggering achievement.

I also wanted to find out more about croissants whilst I was in Paris because, in my opinion, they have declined in quality in France over the last ten years. Some bakeries use mass-produced products instead of baking them fresh on their premises. However, I'm pleased to say that all the bakeries I visited were baking their wares on site and they tasted amazing. For the best croissants in town, I made a beeline for Laurent Duchêne's neighbourhood bakery, on the corner of rue Wurtz and rue Daviel. Look for the sign outside the shop that reads 'Meilleur Ouvrier de France' – Laurent has been named the best baker in France and his award-winning croissants were recognised as the best in the country in 2012. You must buy a couple to see why. They look like any other croissant, but bite into them and they are so buttery and light. I had to find out what Laurent's secret was – read more on page 72. It was great to see that France's speciality product is back to where it should be.

If you fancy a non-touristy trip to Paris, then map your way around, bakery by bakery. Definitely put the two places I've mentioned above on your to-do list, along with Poilâne, for their famous round sourdough loaves. Then head to patisserie Stohrer (the city's oldest) at 51 rue Montorgueil. Du Pain et des Idées, at 34 rue Yves Toudic, and Liberté are within two minutes' walk of each other near Canal Saint-Martin. One is steeped in tradition but with modern ideas like matcha tea-flavoured croissants, the other is sleek with an industrial kitchen on show. Liberté is the bakery that inspired me to include recipes for madeleines (see page 85) and square jammy dodgers (see page 92).

PLAT DU JOUR
VIN AU VERRE

*Lunch*

CHAM
LIQU

*Din*

# CROISSANTS / Makes 12

For me there is nothing better than a warm croissant and a pot of coffee. Especially in Paris, where you can definitely judge a bakery by the quality of their croissants. Whilst I was there, I visited croissant connoisseur Laurent Duchêne for some tips: use the best ingredients you can; always use French butter, as this gives a distinctive rich flavour; keep the dough and the butter at the same temperature; and, when rolling out and creating the layers, make sure the dough and butter are the same thickness.

The recipe below will help you to produce a very good croissant. Maybe not up to Laurent's standards, but definitely up there with the best! It will take you a bit of time, but it will be well worth the effort.

**PREP:** 1 hour

**CHILL:** 8 hours or overnight + 13 hours

**PROVE:** 2 hours

**BAKE:** 15 minutes

350g strong white bread flour, plus extra for dusting

150g plain flour

10g salt

80g caster sugar

10g instant yeast

300ml water

300g unsalted butter (I use Lescure French butter)

1 beaten egg, to glaze

1. Put the flours into the bowl of a mixer fitted with a dough hook. Add the salt and sugar to one side of the bowl and the yeast to the other side. Add the water and mix on a slow speed for 2 minutes. Increase the speed to medium and mix for a further 6 minutes. The dough should come together and be fairly stiff.

2. Tip the dough on to a lightly floured surface and form it into a ball. Place it in a clean bowl, cover with clingfilm and chill in the fridge for 8 hours or overnight.

3. Flatten the butter into a rectangle approximately 40cm x 19cm. Place in the fridge. Take the dough and, on a lightly floured surface, roll it into a rectangle approximately 60cm x 20cm. Place the butter on the dough so it covers the bottom two thirds of it. Ensure that the butter is positioned neatly and comes almost to the edges of the dough.

4. Fold the exposed dough down over one half of the butter. Now cut off the exposed bit of butter without cutting through the dough. Place it on top of the dough you have just folded down. Fold the bottom half of the dough up. Pinch the edges to seal in the butter, then wrap in clingfilm and place in the fridge for an hour to harden.

5. Unwrap the dough and place on a lightly floured surface with one of the short ends towards you. Roll into a rectangle approximately 60cm x 20cm. Fold half the dough upwards away from you, then fold down the other half so they meet in the middle. Then fold the top half over the bottom half. This is called a 'book turn'. Wrap it again and chill for an hour in the fridge. Roll the dough out again and repeat the book turn. Wrap and chill for another hour.

6. When you are ready to shape the croissants, line two or three baking trays with parchment paper. Place the dough on a lightly floured surface and roll into a rectangle approximately 42cm x 30cm x 0.7cm thick. Trim the edges to neaten.

7. Cut the rectangle lengthways, then cut triangles along the length of each strip. The base of each triangle should be 12cm wide and the triangle should be 15cm high. You will get six triangles from each strip.

8. Hold the wide base of a triangle and gently tug the opposite end to cause slight tension in the dough. Now starting at the base, roll each one up into a croissant. As you make them, place the croissants on the prepared trays, allowing room for growth. Put each tray into a clean bag and leave to rise at room temperature for 2 hours or until doubled in size.

9. Preheat your oven to 200°C/Gas 6. Just before baking, egg-wash the croissants. Bake for 15 minutes or until golden. Cool on a wire rack. Best eaten warm.

I COULD HAVE STAYED HERE ALL DAY ...

# QUICHE LORRAINE / Serves 6

Whilst browsing the patisserie windows of Paris, I spotted delicious-looking quiches nestled in alongside pretty, elegant fruit tarts. With not a fluted casing in sight, these quiches all had straight sides and were quite deep. Here is my recipe for the classic quiche Lorraine made with bacon. Real men do eat quiche!

**PREP:** 45 minutes

**CHILL:** 30 minutes

**BAKE:** 40–45 minutes

### for the shortcrust pastry:

225g plain flour, plus extra for dusting

a pinch of fine salt

60g cold unsalted butter, cut roughly into 1cm dice, plus extra for greasing

60g lard, cut roughly into 1cm dice

3–5 tablespoons very cold water

### for the filling:

200g smoked streaky bacon, cut into small lardons

4 medium egg yolks

2 whole medium eggs

500ml double cream

a good pinch of ground white pepper

### equipment:

20cm loose bottom sandwich tin, 4.5–5cm deep

1. To make the pastry, put the flour into a bowl and mix in the salt. Add the butter and lard and rub into the flour using your fingertips, until the mix resembles fine breadcrumbs. Alternatively, you can do this in a food processor or mixer, then transfer to a bowl.

2. Now work in just enough cold water to bring the dough together. When it begins to stick together, gently knead it into a ball. Wrap in clingfilm and chill in the fridge for about 30 minutes.

3. Preheat your oven to 200°C/Gas 6 and have ready a greased 20cm loose bottom sandwich tin, 4.5–5cm deep. Place on a baking tray.

4. Roll out the pastry on a lightly floured surface to a 0.3cm thickness and line the tart tin, leaving the excess overhanging the edge of the tin. Keep a little uncooked pastry back in case you need to patch any cracks later. Prick the base of the pastry with a fork. Line the pastry with parchment paper and fill with baking beans or uncooked rice or lentils.

5. Bake blind for 15 minutes, then remove the parchment and baking beans and return the pastry to the oven for another 8 to 10 minutes, or until it looks dry and faintly coloured. Remove from the oven and leave to cool.

6. Meanwhile, to make the filling, gently fry the bacon over a low to medium heat for about 5 minutes until the fat begins to run and it is cooked through. Set aside to cool.

7. Trim away the excess pastry from the edge of the tin. Use a tiny bit of the reserved uncooked pastry to patch any cracks or holes as necessary. Beat the egg yolks and whole eggs well and add the cream and the pepper. Pour the mixture into the pastry case. Sprinkle over the cooked bacon.

8. Bake for 20 minutes, then reduce the heat to 180°C/Gas 4 and continue to cook for another 20 to 25 minutes until the filling has set and is golden brown.

9. Leave in the tin to cool for 5 minutes, then carefully remove it. This quiche is best served warm or at room temperature. Perfect with a mixed salad.

# ÉCLAIRS / Makes 12

Parisian patisserie windows are fashion statements in their own right. Rows of exquisitely decorated éclairs catch your eye as they glisten like jewels. Chatting to pastry chefs there, I discovered that when making the delicate choux pastry for them, they use a mixture of milk and water as this gives a softer éclair. Just water is used if they are making choux to construct something such as the famous croquembouche tower, as this gives a firmer choux bun.

**PREP:** 25 minutes

**BAKE:** 30–35 minutes

**for the choux pastry:**

125ml full-fat milk

125ml water

125g unsalted butter

2 teaspoons caster sugar

½ teaspoon salt

150g strong white bread flour

4 medium eggs

**for the filling:**

20g hazelnuts

20g almonds

100g mascarpone cheese

300ml double cream

2 tablespoons caster sugar

**for the topping:**

75g caster sugar

25g chopped hazelnuts

250g chocolate fondant icing

50ml liquid glucose

2 tablespoons water

**equipment:**

piping bag fitted with
  a 1cm plain nozzle

1. Preheat your oven to 190°C/Gas 5 and line two baking trays with parchment paper.

2. To make the choux pastry, put the milk, water, butter, sugar and salt into a large saucepan. Heat gently until all the butter has melted, then bring to the boil. Tip in the flour. Beat with a wooden spoon to form a smooth ball of dough that leaves the sides of the pan. This will take a couple of minutes.

3. Transfer the dough to a large bowl. Now vigorously beat the eggs one at a time into the dough. This takes a bit of elbow grease. The dough will become glossy. Stop adding the egg if the dough starts to become loose.

4. Transfer the mixture into a piping bag fitted with a 1cm plain nozzle. Pipe 12 lengths on to the baking trays, allowing room for spreading. Bake for 30 to 35 minutes or until risen, crisp and golden. Remove from the oven and split one side of each éclair to allow the steam to escape. Cool on a wire rack.

5. To make the filling, finely chop the hazelnuts and almonds. Beat the mascarpone until smooth. Whip the cream with the sugar until it holds soft peaks. Combine the nuts with the mascarpone, then fold in the cream. Place in a piping bag with a plain nozzle and fill the éclairs.

6. For the topping, melt the sugar in a pan until it turns a golden caramel colour. Pour on to a baking tray lined with parchment paper. Scatter the chopped hazelnuts on top of the caramel and leave to set. Chop into fine pieces or blitz in a processor to make praline.

7. Place the chocolate fondant icing in a pan with the glucose and water. Heat gently, stirring occasionally, until the icing is soft. Leave the icing to cool a little so it thickens then, using a palette knife, spread the chocolate icing on the top of each éclair. Sprinkle with the praline and enjoy.

VENTE A EMPORTER
PAINS
SPECIAUX
FABRICATION
ARTISANALE

BOULANGER PATISSIER

Pain Bio    La Montmartoise    Sandwiches

Boulangerie    Patisserie
Boulangerie    MURCIANO    Pâtisserie

PANIFICA    BOULANGERIE

FABRICATION ARTISANALE
PAINS AU LEVAIN NATUREL

BOULANGER
La Renaissance

1er Arr
RUE
PASTEUR
WAGNER

OULANGERIE PATI

SPECIAL
de
FOU

PETRI ET CUIT
DANS MON FOURNIL
PAINS
VIENNOISERIES
PATISSERIES

PATISSERIE
STOHRER
MAISON FONDEE
EN 1730

Miche Décorée avec Inscription
Poids : 2,1 kg / Prix pièce : 29,55 €
Sur commande

farine de blé moulue à la meule de
pierre, eau, sel de Guérande

Miche Poilâ
4,79 € / k

# MADELEINES / Makes 20–24

These shell-shaped buttery cakes are found in bakeries all over Paris. They are perfect to nibble with a cup of tea. Whilst it's not traditional, I like to make mine with a brown butter, which gives a toasted nutty flavour and pretty speckled effect throughout the cakes.

**PREP:** 25 minutes

**BAKE:** 8–10 minutes

100g unsalted butter, plus extra for greasing

2 medium eggs

100g caster sugar

1 teaspoon vanilla extract

100g plain flour, plus extra for dusting

½ teaspoon bicarbonate of soda

icing sugar, to sprinkle

**equipment:**

2 madeleine baking trays (or reuse if you have only one)

1.  Place the butter in a pan and heat gently. Once it has melted, continue cooking until it turns golden brown and flecks start to appear. Remove from the heat and leave to cool.

2.  Preheat your oven to 200°C/Gas 6. Grease the madeleine baking trays with butter, then dust with a little flour. Tap the tray to remove any excess flour.

3.  Beat the eggs, caster sugar and vanilla extract until the sugar has dissolved and the mixture is light and fluffy. Sift the flour and bicarbonate of soda into the egg mix and gently fold until it's all incorporated. Pour in the brown butter and mix gently. Leave the batter to stand for 15 minutes.

4.  Fill each madeleine mould to three quarters full with the batter. Place the tray in the oven and bake for 8 to 10 minutes until the madeleines have risen and the centre is cooked. These are best eaten fresh the same day, sprinkled with icing sugar.

# FIG AND APRICOT TART /

Serves 6–8

When in Paris it is hard not to notice the rows of individual, brightly coloured fruit tarts on offer in the city's patisseries. Crisp, sweet pastry filled with vanilla custard or crème pâtissière and beautifully glazed adornments of fruit – a real treat.

**PREP:** 45 minutes

**BAKE:** 50–55 minutes

**for the pastry:**

200g plain flour

2 tablespoons icing sugar

100g cold unsalted butter, diced

1 medium egg

2–3 teaspoons ice-cold water

**for the crème pâtissière:**

450ml full-fat milk

1 vanilla pod

4 large egg yolks

5 tablespoons caster sugar

4 tablespoons cornflour

**for the topping:**

8 ripe apricots, 7 halved and 1 quartered

6 ripe figs, quartered

1 tablespoon demerara sugar

3 tablespoons mixed berry jam, to glaze

**equipment:**

23cm loose bottom tart tin

1. To make the pastry, sift the flour and icing sugar into a bowl and mix well. Add the butter and rub it in lightly with your fingertips until the mixture resembles fine breadcrumbs. Mix the egg with 2 teaspoons of the water. Add to the mixture and stir, adding another teaspoon of water if necessary. When the dough begins to stick together, gently knead it into a smooth ball. Wrap the pastry in clingfilm and chill for at least 30 minutes.

2. Preheat the oven to 200°C/Gas 6. Roll out the pastry on a lightly floured surface to about 3mm thick and use it to line a 23cm loose bottom tart tin, leaving a little excess pastry hanging over the edge. Prick the base of the pastry with a fork, cover with a sheet of parchment paper and fill with baking beans or uncooked rice or lentils. Bake blind for 12 to 15 minutes, until the pastry is dry to the touch, then remove the parchment and baking beans and return the pastry case to the oven for about 5 minutes until it is very lightly coloured. Use a small, sharp knife to trim away the excess pastry from the edge.

3. To make the crème pâtissière, place the milk in a saucepan. Scrape the seeds from the vanilla pod and place the seeds and pod in the pan with the milk. Slowly bring the milk to the boil.

4. In a mixing bowl, beat the egg yolks, caster sugar and cornflour together. As soon as the milk boils, pour half on to the egg mixture and whisk. Return this to the pan with the remaining milk and stir continuously over a low heat for about 2 minutes until the mixture thickens. As it begins to come to the boil, remove from the heat and place in a clean bowl. Cover the surface with clingfilm and leave to go cold. Store in the fridge until required.

5. Preheat the oven to 200°C/Gas 6. Spread the cold crème pâtissière on to the baked tart case. Arrange the apricot halves around the edge of the tart, cut-side up. Place all except one of the fig quarters in a circle inside the apricots, points poking upwards. Next, make a small circle with the apricot quarters; again, the points should be poking upwards. Finally, place a fig quarter in the centre of the tart.

6. Sprinkle the demerara sugar over the fruit. Bake for 15 minutes, then lower the heat to 160°C/Gas 3 and continue baking for 35 to 40 minutes. The edges of the fruit should just be beginning to darken and caramelise. Place on a wire rack to cool. Heat the jam in a small saucepan over a low heat with a splash of water and whilst the tart is still warm, brush over the fruit to glaze.

# CHÂTAIGNE / Makes 1 loaf

Chestnut flour is a really interesting ingredient to use in a loaf of bread as it gives a slightly sweet flavour and a great dark colour once it has been baked. In times past, chestnut flour would have been used on its own by peasants, firstly in Europe and later in America, as chestnuts were cheap and easy to grind. If you make a 100 per cent chestnut flour bread, it will be completely gluten-free, but it won't rise as much as a normal wheat-flour loaf. I've decided to use a combination of both types of flours in this recipe. In France it's called a *châtaigne* and it usually looks like a hedgehog, with spiky points along the top. You can try doing this, or simply shape it into a round cob-style loaf.

**PREP:** 20 minutes

**PROVE:** 24 hours (for the starter) + 2–5 hours

**BAKE:** 30 minutes

### for the starter:

250g strong white bread flour

5g instant yeast

175ml water

oil, for greasing

### for the dough:

300g strong white bread flour, plus extra for dusting

200g chestnut flour

7g salt

240–260ml water

1. Begin by making the starter. Place the 250g of bread flour in a bowl with the yeast. Slowly add the water and, with your hand, move the flour around until you've picked up all the flour from around the bowl. The dough will be rough and sticky at this stage.

2. Coat your work surface with a little oil, tip the dough on to it and begin to knead. Work through the initial wet stage until the dough is soft and smooth. This will take around 10 minutes. Place the dough in a clean bowl. Cover and leave to prove for 24 hours in the fridge.

3. Scrape the starter into the bowl of a mixer fitted with a dough hook. Add the 300g bread flour, chestnut flour, salt and three quarters of the water and mix on a slow speed to bring all the ingredients together. Add enough of the remaining water to incorporate all the ingredients. Increase the speed to medium and mix for 5 minutes until you have a smooth, soft dough. Cover and leave to prove until doubled in size – this will take between 1 and 3 hours.

4. Lightly dust your work surface with flour, turn out the dough and fold it in on itself to knock out the air. Shape the dough into a round cob. Place on a baking tray lined with parchment paper. Place the tray in a clean plastic bag and leave to prove until doubled in size – this will take 1 to 2 hours.

5. Preheat your oven to 220°C/Gas 7 and put a roasting tin in the bottom to heat up.

6. Just before baking, dust the surface of the loaf with a little flour. Using scissors, snip randomly over the surface to create points. Fill the hot roasting tin with hot water; this will create steam and help the crust form on the bread. Put the bread into the oven and bake for 30 minutes or until the bread is a rich brown colour and sounds hollow when tapped on the base. Leave to cool completely on a wire rack.

# BRIOCHE / Makes 12 small or 6 medium

Although a sweet dough, brioche has the texture of a cake rather than bread. It's enriched with eggs and butter, which gives it a distinctive yellow crumb. It can be eaten for breakfast and with afternoon tea, but can also be enjoyed toasted and served with terrines and pâtés.

**PREP:** 25 minutes

**CHILL:** 7 hours

**PROVE:** 2–3 hours

**BAKE:** 15–20 minutes

350g strong white bread flour, plus extra for dusting

5g salt

35g caster sugar

7g instant yeast

80ml warm full-fat milk

3 medium eggs

170g softened unsalted butter, plus extra for greasing

1 beaten egg, to glaze

### equipment:

12 small (7.5cm) or 6 medium-sized (11cm) brioche moulds

1. Put the flour into the bowl of a mixer fitted with a dough hook. Add the salt and sugar to one side of the bowl and the yeast to the other.

2. Add the milk and eggs and mix on a slow speed for 2 minutes, then on a medium speed for a further 6 to 8 minutes until you have a soft, glossy elastic dough.

3. Add the softened butter and continue to mix for a further 4 to 5 minutes, scraping down the bowl periodically to ensure that the butter is fully incorporated. The dough will be very soft.

4. Tip the dough into a bowl, cover and chill overnight or for at least 7 hours until it is firm and you are able to shape it.

5. Grease 12 small (7.5cm) or 6 medium-sized (11cm) brioche moulds with butter. Take the brioche dough from the fridge. Tip it on to a lightly floured surface and fold it in on itself a few times to knock out the air. Divide it up into 6 or 12 equal pieces, depending on the size of the moulds you are using. Pinch a grape-sized piece from each ball to use as the top knot.

6. Shape each larger piece into a smooth ball by placing it into a cage formed by your hand and the table and moving your hand around in a circular motion, rotating the ball rapidly. Do the same with the smaller pieces. Make a hole in the middle of the larger balls of dough and stretch the hole so the ball looks like a tall doughnut.

7. Shape the smaller balls into cylinders and taper one end of them. From the tapered end, cut the cylinders halfway up and pull the two parts apart. Feed the tapered ends through the hole in the large ball and tuck underneath. Form the top of the cylinder into a ball.

8. Put the dough into the moulds on a baking tray, then cover with a clean plastic bag and leave to prove for 2 to 3 hours or until doubled in size.

9. Preheat your oven to 190°C/Gas 5.

10. Before baking your brioche, brush each one with the egg wash. Bake for 15 to 20 minutes until risen and golden brown. Bear in mind that the sugar and the butter will make the brioche colour up before it is fully baked, so check that they are done by carefully tipping one out of its mould and tapping the bottom. It should sound hollow when done.

11. Remove your brioche buns from their moulds and let them cool on a wire rack.

# FRENCH SQUARE JAMMY DODGERS / Makes 6

I spotted these large square biscuits in the window of a patisserie called Liberté and thought they looked fun. They are made using the classic French pâte sablée or 'sweet pastry', which is rich and buttery. The pastry is very short so it's important to let it rest; this makes it easier to handle. Raspberry jam works well, but you can try other jams instead.

**PREP:** 20 minutes

**CHILL:** 30 minutes

**BAKE:** 12–14 minutes

275g plain flour, plus extra for dusting

220g unsalted butter, cut into dice

100g icing sugar, sifted

a pinch of salt

2 medium egg yolks

140g seedless raspberry jam

**equipment:**

9cm and 4.5cm square cutters

1. Place the flour, butter, icing sugar and salt in a mixing bowl. Rub together until the mixture resembles breadcrumbs. Add the egg yolks and bring together to form a ball.

2. On a lightly floured surface, knead gently to form a smooth ball of dough. Wrap this in clingfilm and place in the fridge for at least 30 minutes.

3. Line two baking trays with parchment paper.

4. On a lightly floured surface, roll out the dough to 0.5cm thick. Using a 9cm square cutter, cut out 12 squares. You will need to re-roll the trimmings. Using a 4.5cm square cutter, make a square hole in the middle of six of the large square biscuits. Place the biscuits on the prepared trays and put into in the fridge to rest for 30 minutes.

5. Preheat your oven to 170°C/Gas 3.

6. Bake the biscuits for 12 to 14 minutes until pale and just beginning to colour, but cooked through. The biscuits will be soft whilst warm, so leave on the trays for a few minutes until they have set, then transfer to a wire rack to cool.

7. Once cooled, take the whole biscuits and turn them upside down. Place a dollop of jam in the middle of each one. Spread it out a little, being careful not to go to the edges. Top each one with a biscuit with a hole in and gently push together.

# BAGUETTES / Makes 4

France has a very strong bread culture, with bakeries found on most street corners. The French buy their bread twice daily. By law in France, bakeries must close one day a week, so those in each neighbourhood will schedule their days off to ensure that there is always fresh bread available.

You may not have considered making baguettes before, so this is one to try if you fancy having a go and don't mind spending some time on it. This baguette recipe is very authentic, but you do need to give it two lots of 24-hour proving. Don't let this put you off: the slow prove gives fantastic flavour and you'll end up with perfect French baguettes.

**PREP:** 50 minutes

**PROVE:** 48 hours

**BAKE:** 20 minutes

olive oil, for greasing

500g strong white bread flour, plus extra for dusting

10g salt

3g instant yeast

320–340ml cool water

**equipment:**

2–3 litre rectangular plastic container (it's important to use a rectangular tub as it will help shape the dough) and a baguette tray or 2 baking trays

1.  Lightly oil the 2–3 litre rectangular plastic container.

2.  To make the dough, put the flour into the bowl of a mixer fitted with a dough hook. Add the salt to one side and the yeast to the other and begin mixing on a slow speed. Gradually add the water and as the dough starts to come together continue to mix on a slow speed for 5 minutes, then increase the speed to medium and mix for 10 to 15 minutes until you have a glossy, very elastic dough. When pulled, the dough should stretch so it's almost transparent without breaking. If it breaks, mix for another 5 minutes. Tip the dough into the prepared tub, then cover and leave to prove for 24 hours in the fridge.

3.  Line two baking trays with parchment paper or use a baguette tray. Coat the work surface with a little olive oil, then carefully tip the dough on to it. Rather than knocking it back, handle it gently so you keep as much air in the dough as possible. This helps to create the irregular, airy texture of a really good baguette. The dough will be wet to the touch but still lively.

4.  Divide the dough into four pieces. Shape each piece into an oblong by flattening the dough out slightly and folding the sides up into the middle. Roll each oblong up into a sausage – the top should be smooth with a join running along the length of the base. Now, beginning in the middle, roll out each sausage to the length of your baguette or baking trays with your hands. Don't force it out by pressing heavily. Concentrate on the backwards and forwards movement and gently use the weight of your arms to roll out the dough. Place the baguettes on the prepared trays and put each into a clean plastic bag, leaving them to prove for 24 hours in the fridge.

5.  Preheat your oven to 220°C/Gas 7 and put a roasting tin into the bottom of it to heat up. When the baguettes have risen, dust them lightly with flour and slash each one three times along its length on the diagonal with a sharp knife.

6.  Fill the roasting tray with hot water – this will create steam and help form a crust on the baguettes. Put the baguettes on the baking trays into the oven. Bake for 20 minutes or until the bread is golden brown and sounds hollow when tapped on the bottom. Cool on a wire rack.

# PEAR AND ALMOND TART /

Serves 6

Pear and almond go so well together, especially in this tart. You will get sweet, chewy frangipane encasing the soft, subtle flavour of the pears and the short pastry holds it all together. Easy to make, it's a winner for serving at dinner parties. Perfect served with cream or ice cream.

**PREP:** 1 hour

**CHILL:** 30 minutes

**BAKE:** 40–45 minutes

**for the pastry:**

170g plain flour, plus extra for dusting

30g ground almonds

2 tablespoons icing sugar

100g cold unsalted butter, cut into small pieces

1 medium egg

2–3 teaspoons ice-cold water

**for the filling:**

150g unsalted butter

150g caster sugar

3 medium eggs

75g plain flour

115g ground almonds

½ teaspoon almond essence

3 ripe dessert pears, peeled, halved and cored

a few whole blanched almonds

**to assemble:**

75g apricot glaze or apricot jam

edible gold leaf

**equipment:**

20cm x 30cm loose bottom tart tin

1.  To make the pastry, place the flour, ground almonds and icing sugar in a bowl and mix well. Add the butter and rub it in lightly with your fingertips until the mixture resembles fine breadcrumbs. Mix the egg with 2 teaspoons of the water. Add to the mixture and stir, adding another teaspoon of water if necessary. When the dough begins to stick together, gently knead it into a smooth ball. Wrap the pastry in clingfilm and chill for at least 30 minutes.

2.  Preheat the oven to 200°C/Gas 6. Roll out the pastry on a lightly floured surface to about 3mm thick and use it to line a 20cm x 30cm loose bottom tart tin, leaving a little excess pastry hanging over the edge. Line the pastry case with a sheet of parchment paper and fill with baking beans or uncooked rice or lentils. Bake blind for 12 to 15 minutes, until the pastry is dry to the touch, then remove the parchment and baking beans and return the pastry case to the oven for about 5 minutes, until it is very lightly coloured. Use a small, sharp knife to trim away the excess pastry from the edge.

3.  To make the frangipane filling, beat the butter and caster sugar together until light and fluffy, then beat in the eggs, one at a time. Stir in the flour, ground almonds and the almond essence.

4.  Spread the frangipane on to the baked tart case. Slice the pear halves lengthways (not all the way through) to create a fan effect and arrange them, cut-side down, on top of the frangipane. Arrange the blanched almonds around the pears. Bake in the oven for 15 minutes, then lower the heat to 160°C/Gas 3 and bake for 25 to 30 minutes. The pears should be golden brown and the frangipane should have risen round the fruit.

5.  Place the tart on a wire rack to cool. Heat the apricot glaze or jam with a little water and, whilst the tart is still warm, brush over the fruit to glaze. Decorate the tart with the gold leaf.

# CHOCOLATE AND HAZELNUT MERINGUES / Makes 4–6

Giant meringues are real showstoppers and crowd pleasers. The method is a little different from a regular meringue, but the ingredients are the same – just egg whites and sugar. Always weigh your egg whites as this will give you more accurate results. Heating them gently with the sugar until it dissolves helps achieve a very crisp set to the meringues. The chocolate and hazelnuts give a great flavour combination.

**PREP:** 20 minutes

**BAKE:** 1¼ hours

150g egg whites (4 or 5 eggs, depending on size)

200g caster sugar

10g cocoa powder

25g chopped hazelnuts

optional: whipped cream and berries, to serve

1. Preheat the oven to 120°C/Gas ½ and line two large baking trays with parchment paper.

2. Place the egg whites and sugar in a large bowl over a pan of simmering water. Using a balloon whisk, mix until the sugar has dissolved and the mix is warm but not too hot to touch (you don't want to start cooking the egg whites). Now transfer to an electric stand mixer and whisk for about 10 minutes until the meringue has thickened, is glossy and has cooled. If you don't have a stand mixer, use an electric whisk – just make sure the bowl is large.

3. Sift half the cocoa powder over the meringue and stir gently to create a ripple effect. Repeat using the remaining cocoa. Spoon four or six little mounds of meringue on to each tray. Scatter the hazelnuts over them, then place the trays in the oven and bake for 2 hours. When done, turn the oven off and leave the meringues to go cold and dry out completely; overnight is best.

4. These meringues are lovely served in a large bowl in the centre of the table with soft whipped cream and berries.

# PUDDING LANE /

## LONDON

Individual gala pies / Scones / Lemon drizzle slices /
Victoria sponge / Iced cherry fingers / Steak and kidney pie /
Chelsea buns / Slow-fermented white tin loaf /
Battenberg / Sausage rolls

There is such a rich history of baking in London and the rest of the UK that I can't possibly fit it all in here. Instead, I want to look at a few key moments that have defined British baking. We all know the story of the Great Fire of London starting at Thomas Farriner's bakery in the aptly named Pudding Lane in 1666, so I had to name this chapter after that. Although back then, 'pudding' referred to the offal that would fall off the carts on their way to the docks, instead of the delicious bakes we eat as puddings these days.

Also in 1666, Cliveden House was built just outside London. One of the UK's finest country houses, it serves a fantastic afternoon tea. I used to work in the kitchens at Cliveden so wanted to venture back there to take a look at some of the classic cakes they serve today. For afternoon tea you can expect to enjoy an array of finger sandwiches, a variety of cakes from Victoria sponge to lemon drizzle (see pages 123 and 118) and the classic scone – the hero of the British cream tea. My recipe on page 114 provides three different flavours: plain, walnut and fruit.

Also at the top end of the spectrum for an afternoon tea is the iconic food emporium Fortnum & Mason, which now has a top-floor tea room – elegant and steeped in tradition. A sanctuary away from the crowds on Piccadilly below, the Diamond Jubilee Tea Salon is definitely worth a visit. My recipe for iced cherry finger buns on page 124 is a tribute to it.

There are so many exciting things happening in London on the food scene right now. Borough Market has long been showcasing new producers and products and a recent addition there is Bread Ahead, run by Matt Jones and Justin Gellatly. It has taken them 10 years to perfect their sourdough bread, which is one of the best I've ever tasted. I enjoyed an afternoon of baking with Matt and you can too, as they run an on-site bakery course that is open to the public. Every day their fresh loaves and signature doughnuts are sold across the road at their Bread Ahead stall in the market building.

From the upper-class tea rooms of the West End, to the foodie heartbeat of Borough, I then travelled to the East End – perfect pie and pint territory. It's definitely worth checking out the Marksman pub on Hackney Road, run by Jon Rotherham, who has a pie of the day on his seasonal menu. I like to keep things classic, so the recipe I've given you on page 127 is for my favourite steak and kidney pie.

# INDIVIDUAL GALA PIES / Makes 12

We Brits love our pies, in any shape or form, so it will come as no surprise that I'm very partial to them! I particularly love these mini gala pies with the hidden gem of a quail's egg nestled inside each one. Perfect picnic food or served as part of a ploughman's.

**PREP:** 35 minutes

**BAKE:** 40 minutes

**for the filling:**

300g good-quality sausage meat (or skinned sausages)

300g pork mince

150g unsmoked bacon, diced

2 banana shallots, finely diced

½ teaspoon ground mace

½ teaspoon nutmeg

½ teaspoon dried sage

salt and ground white pepper

12 quail's eggs, hard-boiled and peeled

**for the pastry:**

450g plain flour, plus extra for dusting

100g strong white bread flour

75g cold unsalted butter

200ml water

½ teaspoon salt

100g lard, plus extra for greasing

2 beaten egg yolks, to glaze

**for the jelly:**

1 chicken stock cube

300ml boiling water

3 leaves of gelatine

**equipment:**

10cm round cutter

12-hole muffin tin

1. Preheat your oven to 200°C/Gas 6. Grease a 12-hole muffin tin with lard.

2. Begin by making the filling. Put all the ingredients, except the boiled quail's eggs, into a large bowl. Season with salt and a pinch of white pepper. Use your hands to mix together thoroughly. Fry off a nugget of the mixture and taste to check the seasoning. Add a little more if required. Place the mix in the fridge whilst you make the pastry.

3. Place the flours in a bowl. Add the butter and rub in lightly with your fingertips. Heat the water, salt and lard in a small pan until just boiling. Pour on to the flours and mix together with a wooden spoon. Once cool enough to handle, tip on to a lightly floured surface and knead to a smooth dough.

4. Roll the pastry out to a thickness of about 3mm. Cut out twelve 10cm circles and use each circle to line a hole in the muffin tin. Cut twelve 7cm circles for the lids and set them aside.

5. Spoon a little of the mixture into each pie case, place a quail's egg in the centre and spoon over a little more filling. Brush the edge of each pie case with a little egg yolk, place the lids on top and crimp the edges together to seal completely. Make a small hole in the centre of each pie and bake in the oven for 40 minutes, until the pastry is crisp and golden. Leave to cool in the tin for 10 minutes, then remove and cool on a wire rack.

6. Make the jelly by melting the stock cube in the boiling water. Soak the gelatine in a little cold water until soft, then squeeze out any excess water and whisk into the warm chicken stock. Pour the jelly mixture into the hole in the top of each pie until the hollow cavity in the pie is filled. Allow the pies to set in the fridge overnight.

# SCONES / Makes 15

During my time working in some of the UK's finest hotels, I have made thousands of scones. Being back in the kitchens at Cliveden House making afternoon tea was great fun. It was there that I learnt that the 'correct' way to stamp out scones was using a straight cutter as a crinkly one was for the lower classes!

My scone recipe uses strong bread flour; this gives a great structure to the dough and creates a fluffy light crumb in the finished scone. The basic recipe here can be adapted to include many different flavours. I've given instructions below for walnut scones and fruit scones, but feel free to let your imagination wander and experiment with your favourite flavours. The question of whether you like to spread your jam or your cream on first will determine whether you prefer a Cornish (jam first) or Devon (cream first) cream tea.

**PREP:** 15 minutes

**BAKE:** 12–15 minutes

500g strong white bread flour, plus extra for dusting

5 teaspoons baking powder

80g softened unsalted butter

80g caster sugar

2 medium eggs

250ml full-fat milk

1 beaten egg, to glaze

**for walnut scones:**

add 100g chopped walnuts

**for fruit scones:**

add 100g sultanas

**equipment:**

5.5cm round cutter

1. Preheat your oven to 220°C/Gas 7. Line two baking trays with parchment paper.

2. Place the flour, baking powder, butter and sugar in a mixing bowl. Rub the ingredients together with your fingers to form a breadcrumb-like mixture. Add the eggs and turn the mixture gently to incorporate the ingredients. Add half the milk and keep turning the mixture to combine. A little at a time, add the remaining milk to form a soft dough.

3. Place the dough on a lightly floured surface. Use your hands to fold the dough in half, then turn it 90 degrees and repeat. Do this a few times until the dough is smooth. (If you are making flavoured scones, add the walnuts or sultanas now.) Keep dusting the work surface with flour if the dough is sticking. Do not overwork the dough.

4. Roll the dough to 2.5cm thick. Using a 5.5cm round cutter dipped in flour, stamp out rounds and place them on the prepared trays. Try not to twist the cutter, just press down then lift up and press out the dough. Re-roll any offcuts and cut out more scones. Leave them to rest for a few minutes, then brush each one with egg wash, being careful not to let the egg run down the sides.

5. Bake the scones for 12 to 15 minutes, until golden and well risen. Leave to cool, then split in half and enjoy with butter or clotted cream and jam.

# LEMON DRIZZLE SLICES /

Makes 12

I am partial to a slice of lemon drizzle and that's why I decided to include it in the afternoon tea that I served at Cliveden House during my visit back there. This cake is decorated with a feather icing and it looks really impressive, but it's incredibly easy to make. I like to serve it in slices.

**PREP:** 15 minutes

**BAKE:** 25–30 minutes

### for the cake:

70g softened unsalted butter

120g caster sugar

2 medium eggs

140g self-raising flour

1 teaspoon baking powder

1 lemon, finely zested

1 tablespoon lemon curd

2 tablespoons full-fat milk

### for the drizzle topping:

30g granulated sugar

juice of 1 lemon

### for the feather icing:

250g icing sugar

3 tablespoons water

a splash of yellow food colouring

### equipment:

20cm square baking tin and a disposable icing bag

1. Preheat your oven to 180°C/Gas 4. Line a 20cm x 20cm square baking tin with parchment paper.

2. Using an electric whisk, beat the butter and caster sugar together until pale, light and fluffy. Add the eggs and mix again. Add the flour, baking powder, lemon zest, lemon curd and milk and mix with a wooden spoon until all the ingredients are thoroughly combined. Pour the mixture into the prepared tin and bake for 25 to 30 minutes or until a skewer comes out clean.

3. Mix the granulated sugar and lemon juice together and pour over the hot cake. Leave to cool in the tin. You can then eat the cake just as it is, or for a fancy finish try making this feather icing.

4. Mix the icing sugar with just enough of the water to give a runny, but not watery, icing. Take a small amount of icing and place it in a separate bowl. Add a few drops of the food colouring to this icing until you have the desired colour. Spoon this into a disposable icing bag.

5. Remove the cake from the tin and peel off the parchment paper. Sit the cake on a wire rack over a baking tray. Spread the white icing over the cake. Using the icing bag, pipe lines of the coloured icing across the width of the cake. Using a cocktail stick, drag through the lines at right angles to create a feathered effect. Leave to set before cutting into 12 slices.

# VICTORIA SPONGE / Serves 8–10

This is a delicious British teatime classic. I like to add whipped cream to the filling to make it really special, but if you are a traditionalist then just sandwich the layers together with jam. This recipe uses the old-fashioned way of measuring the ingredients. The flour, sugar and butter should each weigh the same as the four eggs in their shells.

**PREP:** 15 minutes

**BAKE:** 20–25 minutes

### for the sponge:

4 medium eggs

the weight of the eggs
  in softened unsalted butter,
  plus extra for greasing

the weight of the eggs
  in caster sugar

the weight of the eggs
  in plain flour

2 teaspoons baking powder

### to decorate:

100g raspberry jam
  (use more, if you like)

150ml whipping cream

icing or caster sugar,
  for dusting

### equipment:

two 20cm cake tins

1. Preheat your oven to 180°C/Gas 4. Line the base of two 20cm cake tins with parchment paper and lightly butter the sides.

2. Cream the butter and caster sugar together until light and fluffy. Add the eggs one at a time, beating well.

3. Add the flour and baking powder and fold into the mixture until fully incorporated. Divide the mixture between the prepared cake tins.

4. Bake in the centre of the oven for 20 to 25 minutes. The sponge is ready when the top is golden and has slightly shrunk from the sides of the tins. Leave to cool in the tins for a few minutes before moving to a wire rack to cool.

5. Choose the best-looking sponge as your top layer, then lay the other one – top-side down – on your serving plate. Spread the jam over the bottom layer, and then whip the cream to soft peaks and spread over the jam. Place the other layer on top and dust with icing or caster sugar.

# ICED CHERRY FINGERS /

I adore iced finger buns, so I just had to include my recipe in this chapter. The twist I've given to them is to include morello cherries in the dough and a cherry flavour to the icing. Tart and sweet at the same time, with a lovely texture to the actual bun itself – I hope you enjoy making these.

**PREP:** 25 minutes

**PROVE:** 1¾ hours

**BAKE:** 12–14 minutes

**for the dough:**

500g strong white bread flour, plus extra for dusting

40g caster sugar

40g softened unsalted butter

2 teaspoons salt

10g instant yeast

150ml full-fat milk

150ml water

150g glacé morello cherries, finely chopped

**for the icing:**

200g icing sugar

optional: 1–2 tablespoons cherry-flavoured powder

25–30ml cold water

**for the filling:**

200ml double cream, whipped

**equipment:**

piping bag fitted with a small star nozzle

1. To make the dough, place the flour, caster sugar and butter in a large bowl. Add the salt to one side and the yeast to the other. Add the milk and three quarters of the water. Turn the mixture with the fingers of one hand. Add the remaining water a little at a time, mixing until you have incorporated all the flour and the dough is soft and sticky.

2. Lightly flour your work surface. Tip the dough on to it and knead well for 5 to 10 minutes until the surface is smooth. Return the dough to the bowl, cover and leave to rise for 1 hour or until doubled in size.

3. Line a baking tray with parchment paper.

4. Scrape the dough out of the bowl on to a lightly floured surface and fold it inwards repeatedly until all the air has been knocked out. Add the chopped cherries and knead into the dough. Divide the dough into 12 equal pieces. Roll each piece into a ball, then shape into fingers approximately 10cm long.

5. Place the dough fingers on the prepared baking tray, about 7cm apart, leaving space for them to rise but just touch when cooking. Prove for approximately 40 minutes or until doubled in size. Preheat the oven to 220°C/Gas 7.

6. Bake in the oven for 10 to 12 minutes. Place on a wire rack to cool.

7. For the icing, sift the icing sugar and cherry powder, if using, into a large bowl and gradually stir in the cold water to form a thick paste. Take a cooled finger bun and turn it upside down to dip the top of it into the icing, then smooth with a palette knife. Leave to set on a wire rack.

8. Put the cream into a piping bag fitted with a small star nozzle. Slice the iced fingers horizontally, leaving one long edge intact. Pipe a generous line of the cream into the middle of each bun.

# STEAK AND KIDNEY PIE /

Serves 4–6

This is an absolute classic British favourite that has been enjoyed by generations of families, including mine. For me, pies are real comfort food, and steak and kidney is the absolute king. With its soft melting steak and rich gravy, it's a hard one to beat. Do use ox kidney as it can stand the long cooking, rather than lamb's or pig's.

**PREP:** 25 minutes

**COOK:** 1½–2 hours

**CHILL:** 30 minutes

**BAKE:** 30–40 minutes

### for the filling:

3 tablespoons vegetable oil

1 large onion, peeled and chopped

750g braising steak (chuck steak), cut into 4cm chunks

3 tablespoons plain flour

salt and ground white pepper

250g ox kidney, core removed and cut into bite-sized pieces

250g chestnut mushrooms, cut in half

600ml beef stock

a few drops of Worcestershire sauce

1 bay leaf

### for the pastry:

275g plain flour, plus extra for dusting

a pinch of salt

70g cold unsalted butter,

65g cold lard

1 medium egg

2–3 tablespoons cold water

1 beaten egg, to glaze

### equipment:

1.2 litre pie dish

1. Heat 1 tablespoon of the oil in a heavy-based saucepan and fry the onion over a medium heat until soft and just beginning to colour. Remove from the pan and set to one side. Add the rest of the oil to the pan.

2. Toss the steak in the flour and season with a little salt and white pepper. Tap to remove any excess flour and then brown the meat in batches over a medium to high heat. Remove the meat and set to one side. Brown the kidney pieces in the same pan, then remove and set to one side whilst you brown the mushrooms.

3. Return the onion, steak and kidney to the pan. Pour in the stock, Worcestershire sauce and bay leaf. Stir, then bring to a simmer. Cover and cook on a low heat for 1½ to 2 hours until the meat is tender and the sauce reduced. Taste to check the seasoning and add more salt and pepper if needed. Transfer the filling to a 1.2 litre pie dish and leave to cool completely.

4. To make the pastry, mix the flour and salt together. Dice the butter and lard and rub in with your fingers until it looks like breadcrumbs. Beat the egg with the water. Make a well in the centre of the flour mixture and pour in the egg mix. Use a knife to mix together and form a dough. If the dough is too dry, add a splash more water. Turn out on to a lightly floured surface and knead to form a smooth dough. Wrap in clingfilm and leave in the fridge to chill for at least 30 minutes.

5. Preheat the oven to 200°C/Gas 6.

6. On a lightly floured surface, roll out the pastry to a 5–6mm thickness. Cut a 2cm strip of pastry. Dampen the edges of the rim of the pie dish with water. Stick the pastry strip on to the rim and dampen this too. Lay the remaining pastry on top. Press down to seal, then crimp or flute the edges of the pastry and trim off the excess.

7. Just before baking, egg wash the pastry. Bake for 30 to 40 minutes until the pastry is golden brown. Leave to stand for 10 to 15 minutes before serving.

# CHELSEA BUNS / Makes 9

These deliciously plump, sweet, sticky, square-shaped spiced buns originated from the Chelsea Bun House in London in the eighteenth century. The trick to getting their square shape is to place the pieces of dough in the baking tin with just enough space between them so, when they prove, the buns will touch each other and batch together once baked. I love to glaze mine with apricot jam for a little extra sweet stickiness.

**PREP:** 25 minutes

**PROVE:** 2½–3½ hours

**BAKE:** 20–25 minutes

**for the dough:**

300ml full-fat milk

40g unsalted butter, plus extra for greasing

500g strong white bread flour, plus extra for dusting

7g salt

7g instant yeast

1 medium egg

olive oil, for greasing

**for the filling:**

25g melted butter

zest of 1 orange

75g light soft brown sugar

1 teaspoon ground cinnamon

a few gratings of fresh nutmeg

100g sultanas

100g currants

100g dried apricots, chopped

**for the glaze:**

75g apricot jam

**equipment:**

24cm square deep roasting tin

1. Place the milk and butter in a small saucepan and heat gently until the butter has melted. Remove from the heat and set to one side.

2. Place the flour in a large mixing bowl and add the salt to one side and the yeast to the other. Add the lukewarm milk and the egg and mix together with one hand to make a rough dough.

3. Generously dust your work surface with flour and begin to knead. Continue kneading for 5 to 10 minutes. Work through the initial wet stage and form a soft dough with a smooth skin. Place in a lightly oiled bowl, cover and leave to rise for 2 to 3 hours or until doubled in size.

4. Grease a 24cm square deep roasting tin with butter and line with parchment paper.

5. Tip the dough on to a lightly floured surface and roll into a rectangle approximately 0.5cm thick. Tack down the edge closest to you by pressing it down on to the work surface with your thumb. Brush the surface with melted butter, then sprinkle over the orange zest, sugar, cinnamon, nutmeg and the dried fruit.

6. Roll from the opposite side of dough towards you as tightly as you can. Cut nine equal pieces and place these in rows of three in the prepared tin, cut-side up. Leave a gap of 1cm between each bun.

7. Cover and leave to prove for 30 minutes. Meanwhile, preheat your oven to 190°C/Gas 5.

8. Bake for 20 to 25 minutes until risen and golden brown. Leave in the tin for a few minutes to cool slightly before transferring to a wire rack. Melt the jam with a little water, then sieve and brush over the buns whilst they are still warm.

# SLOW-FERMENTED WHITE TIN LOAF / Makes 1 large loaf

This loaf is a great one for beginners. If you've not tried making bread before, then have a go at this recipe. It's a basic method and shouldn't give you any trouble. Just don't get impatient – it takes time for the dough to prove as this ensures that the real bread flavour develops.

**PREP:** 35 minutes

**PROVE:** 36 hours

**BAKE:** 30–35 minutes

400g strong white bread flour, plus extra for dusting

8g salt

2g instant yeast

30g softened unsalted butter

250ml cold water

olive oil, for greasing

**equipment:**

1kg loaf tin

1. Place the flour in a large mixing bowl and add the salt to one side and the yeast to the other. Add the butter and three quarters of the water. Turn the mixture round with your fingers, and continue to add the remaining water until all the flour has been incorporated. You may not need to use all the water.

2. Coat your work surface with a little olive oil. Tip the dough on to the surface and knead it for 5 to 10 minutes. Initially the dough will be wet but, as you work it, it will begin to form a dough with a smooth skin. Place the dough in a lightly oiled bowl, cover and leave to prove in the fridge for 24 hours.

3. Grease a 1kg loaf tin with olive oil. Tip the dough on to a lightly floured surface and fold inwards repeatedly until all the air is knocked out. Shape into an oblong by flattening the dough and folding the sides into the middle. Roll up so the top is smooth and you have a join in the middle on the underside. Put the dough into the prepared tin with the join underneath.

4. Place the tin inside a clean plastic bag and leave to prove until it has risen and fills three quarters of the tin. This can take 12 hours depending on the room temperature.

5. Preheat your oven to 220°C/Gas 7 and place a roasting tin in the bottom.

6. Dust the surface of the loaf with flour and then, using a sharp knife, slash the top. Fill the roasting tray with hot water to create steam and place the bread directly on the shelf in the oven.

7. Bake for 30 to 35 minutes, or until the bread is cooked. Remove from the tin and tap the base; it should sound hollow. Cool the loaf on a wire rack.

# BATTENBERG / Serves 8

Sometimes a one-colour cake is just not enough, and this is where a Battenberg comes into its own. You may think it's fiddly to create two cake mixes, but the finished result is so neat and delicate that you will be very proud of yourself. It's a classic cake to serve as part of afternoon tea.

**PREP:** 45 minutes

**BAKE:** 25–30 minutes

**for the cake:**

110g softened unsalted butter, plus extra for greasing

110g caster sugar

110g self-raising flour

½ teaspoon baking powder

25g ground almonds

2 medium eggs

½ teaspoon vanilla extract

pink food colouring

**to assemble:**

100g apricot glaze or apricot jam

225g white marzipan

icing sugar, for dusting

**equipment:**

20cm square shallow cake tin and a metal skewer

1. Preheat your oven to 170°C/Gas 3. Grease the base and sides of a 20cm square shallow cake tin. To create a divide in the tin so the pink and vanilla cake can cook together, cut a piece of parchment-lined foil (you can buy this already lined; if not just use parchment) as wide as the tin, but 8cm longer. Then fold it in half widthways and push up the centre to make a fold. Line the base of the tin with this, ensuring the pleat runs down the middle of the tin, dividing it in two.

2. To make the sponge, use the 'all-in-one' method. By this, I mean put the butter, caster sugar, flour, baking powder, ground almonds, eggs and vanilla extract into a large bowl. Using an electric whisk, beat until the mixture comes together and is smooth. Put half the mixture into a separate bowl and add enough pink food colouring to turn the mixture a strong shade of pink. Spoon the vanilla mixture into one half of the tin and the pink mixture into the other half. Level the surface of each half with a knife.

3. Bake for 25 to 30 minutes or until well risen and cooked through. Cool the cake in the tin for 10 minutes, then transfer it to a wire rack.

4. Heat the apricot glaze with a splash of water and stir until smooth. Trim the edges off the cooled cake and cut it into four equal strips. Lay one vanilla and one pink strip next to each other and use a little of the apricot glaze to stick them together. Spread a bit more glaze on the top. Stick the remaining two strips together with the glaze and place them on top to create a chequerboard effect. Spread a little more glaze over the top of the assembled cake.

5. Roll the marzipan out into a rectangle – do this on a surface dusted with icing sugar. It needs to be wide enough to wrap around the cake, and trimmed to the length of the cake. Place the glazed side of the cake on the marzipan, positioning it so that when you lift up one long side, it perfectly covers one side of the cake.

6. Cover the remaining three sides of the cake with glaze. Roll the cake over in the marzipan, pressing to neatly cover it. Brush the corner join with water to seal it. Turn the cake so the join is now on the bottom. Trim each end of the cake to reveal the chequerboard effect.

7. Heat a metal skewer over a flame until very hot and scorch the top of the cake with long diagonal lines; you will need to keep heating the skewer to do this.

# SAUSAGE ROLLS / Makes 18–20

As well as crisp, flaky pastry, a good sausage roll deserves a tasty meaty filling. I like to buy good-quality sausages and remove the meat from the skins. I then add a few more ingredients to give a great hit of flavour to the filling. Perfect party nibbles or picnic food.

**PREP:** 45 minutes

**CHILL:** 1½ hours

**BAKE:** 20–25 minutes

### for the pastry:

225g plain flour, plus extra for dusting

½ teaspoon salt

200g cold butter, diced

juice of ½ a lemon

180–190ml cold water

1 beaten egg, to glaze

### for the filling:

20g butter

1 red onion, peeled and sliced

450g sausage meat

1 apple, peeled, cored and grated

½ teaspoon dried sage

a dash of Worcestershire sauce

a pinch of ground white pepper

1. Begin by making the pastry. Place the flour, salt and butter in a bowl. Add the lemon juice and three quarters of the water. Gently stir until the mixture binds together, adding the remaining water if necessary. The dough should be lumpy. Don't overwork it – the idea is to keep the lumps of butter in there.

2. Tip the dough on to a floured work surface and flatten it into a rectangle. Roll out into a narrow rectangle about 2.5cm thick. Fold one third of the dough up on itself and the opposite down over that. This is a turn. Wrap in clingfilm and place the pastry in the fridge for at least 30 minutes, although an hour is preferable.

3. Unwrap the pastry and repeat the turn by rolling it at 90 degrees to the first roll, into a rectangle 40cm x 15cm. Fold again, then wrap and chill for another 20 minutes. Do this twice more, chilling the pastry before each turn.

4. Preheat your oven to 200°C/Gas 6. Line two baking trays with parchment paper.

5. To make the filling, melt the butter in a wide-based pan, add the onion slices and stir well. Cut a circle of baking paper the same size as the pan, wet the paper and screw it up, then unwrap and place on the onions. Very gently cook the onions until they are soft and turn a golden caramel colour. Stir every now and again. Be patient, this takes a long time. Remove from the pan and leave to cool slightly.

6. Mix together the caramelised onion, sausage meat, grated apple, sage, Worcestershire sauce and white pepper until well combined.

7. Roll the pastry into a rectangle approximately 55cm x 20cm and trim the edges to neaten. Place the filling along the centre of the pastry in an even cylinder shape. Brush the long ends of the pastry with the egg wash and tightly roll the pastry around the sausage meat. Use a sharp knife to cut it into pieces about 2.5cm long.

8. Place these rolls on the prepared baking trays and brush each one with egg wash. Bake for 20 to 25 minutes until the pastry is crisp, golden and the meat is cooked through. Remove from the oven and leave to cool before eating warm or cold.

# DANISH TASTIES /

## COPENHAGEN

Kransekage / Apricot and passion fruit wholemeal Danish /
Danish cinnamon snails / Seeded rye bread / Chocolate and date
rye bread loaves / Danish raspberry slices / Danish poppy seed pastries

The food scene in Copenhagen is incredibly exciting, boasting not only fifteen Michelin-starred restaurants including Noma – once the number one restaurant in the world – but some incredible local cafés and bakeries. I was keen to find out more about the rich heritage of Danish baking and, more importantly, about their pastries, which are now famous the world over. It was late November when I arrived. It was cold and the whole city was candlelit, with hurricane lamps in the doorways of every establishment, inviting passers-by to stop off and enjoy some *hygge* (cosiness) – a charming Scandinavian concept, which I think we all need to adopt in our lives.

Starting out at Sankt Peder's Bageri, the city's oldest bakery, I was keen to see and taste their famous *onsdagssnegle*, or 'Wednesday snails'. As their name suggests, they are only available on Wednesdays when the owner, Torben Sørensen, and his staff make a few thousand of these cinnamon, butter and iced sugar spiralled pastries. See page 152 for my recipe based on their delicious version. From there it was a short walk to Torvehallerne, the indoor food market on Frederiksborggade, which is definitely worth a visit. It's a feast for the eyes as well as the stomach, with beautiful displays of bread and pastries at Lauras Bakery, the famous open-faced sandwiches made with thin slices of dense rye sourdough called *smørrebrød*, as well as all kinds of hot food stalls, from top-quality porridge and grain-based dishes at Grød to pizza at Gorm's.

Meyers Bageri is also worth a visit. It opened in 2010 on Jægersborggade in the Nørrebro district. Run by Claus Meyer, the co-founder of Noma, it serves a small selection of high-quality organic breads and pastries as well as seven different types of Meyers flour and ready-made dough, which their customers can buy to bake at home. A great little establishment.

A short taxi ride took me to the suburb of Lyngby to meet with Mette Blomsterberg at the bakery and café restaurant that she runs with her husband Henrik. Mette is a judge on the Danish version of *The Great British Bake Off*, so I was looking forward to meeting her and swapping stories! I also wanted to learn how to make a celebratory marzipan cake with her, called *kransekage* (see page 143). With very few ingredients, it is a stunning-looking tower of a cake. Maybe give it a try next Christmas – it will look incredible as a centrepiece.

I loved my mini-break to Copenhagen (including a roller coaster ride or two in the famous Tivoli Gardens!) and I will definitely be going back to enjoy some more of their welcoming hospitality. This chapter is full of Danish classics for you to have a go at making at home.

# KRANSEKAGE / Serves 20

Mette Blomsterberg is the Mary Berry of the Danish *Bake Off*. She was my guide in Copenhagen and introduced me to typical Danish cuisine and culture. The Danes are very laid-back and easy-going. They even have a word, *hygge*, that means 'cosiness' and they create a warm, friendly atmosphere where they enjoy the good things in life with good people. I certainly felt this, and Mette, a highly trained pastry chef and owner of Blomsterbergs Café, was a fantastic host. We had great fun and together we cooked the traditional Christmas *kransekage*.

**PREP:** 45 minutes

**CHILL:** 4 hours

**BAKE:** 10–12 minutes

250g icing sugar, sifted

2 egg whites

750g almond paste (at least 50% ground almond content)

400g pistachios, finely chopped

300g dark chocolate, melted

icing sugar, to serve

1. Place the icing sugar in a bowl, add the egg whites and mix to form a runny paste.

2. Knead the almond paste to soften and flatten into a thick disc shape. Add the icing sugar paste little by little and knead into the almond paste. Keep adding until you have a soft paste. Shape into a ball, then roll into a cylinder. Wrap in clingfilm and place in the fridge for at least 4 hours.

3. Line two large baking trays with parchment paper and preheat your oven to 190°C/Gas 5.

4. Take the dough and cut into four. Roll each piece into a long rope approximately 2cm thick. Place the chopped pistachios in a large baking tray and gently roll the marzipan ropes in the pistachios to coat.

5. Gently tap along the top of each rope with the heel of your hands to slightly flatten. Run a palette knife under to loosen.

6. Begin to cut the ropes into different-length strips. Start by cutting an 8cm length, then a 10cm, then 12cm, and continue in 2cm increments until you have 13 strips. The largest will be 32cm long. Each strip will make a ring, and they will gradually increase in size.

7. To form the rings, fold the strips into a round and push the edges together to seal. Make sure the curved surface is on the outside of the ring. The smaller rings are the hardest to make, so take your time to shape them.

8. Place the rings on the prepared trays. Place a piece of parchment paper on top of each tray of rings. Take an empty tray and sit it on top of the parchment paper and press gently to flatten the top of each ring. Remove the tray and parchment paper and bake the rings for 10 to 12 minutes.

9. Once the rings have cooled, begin to build the tower. Have your serving plate to hand. Take the largest ring and dip the base in the melted chocolate, then place in the centre of the plate. Repeat with the remaining rings until your tower is complete. Dust with icing sugar before serving.

# APRICOT AND PASSION FRUIT WHOLEMEAL DANISH /

Makes 9

When in Copenhagen, it is well worth visiting Lauras Bakery. I went to their Torvehallerne branch in a corner of the indoor food market. Make sure you are not in a rush as there is so much to look at in the market that you could easily spend an hour or so browsing the different things on offer. You will definitely be spoilt for choice at Lauras with their wide range of breads and pastries. They are particularly well known for using wholemeal flour in their bread and pastries, so here's my recipe for a fruity wholemeal Danish.

**PREP:** 1½ hours

**CHILL:** 12 hours

**BAKE:** 15–20 minutes

**for the wholemeal dough:**

315g strong white bread flour, plus extra for dusting

135g strong wholemeal flour

75g caster sugar

7g salt

7g instant yeast

2 medium eggs

75ml cold water

100ml full-fat milk

225g cold unsalted butter

**for the filling:**

4 ripe passion fruit

70g unsalted butter

2 whole medium eggs

2 egg yolks

100g caster sugar

juice of ½ a lime

1 tin of apricot halves, drained

50g apricot glaze or apricot jam

1. Place both the flours in the bowl of a mixer fitted with a dough hook. Put the sugar and salt at one side and the yeast at the other. Add the eggs, water and milk. Begin mixing on a slow speed for a couple of minutes to bring the ingredients together. Once combined, increase the speed and mix for 5 minutes.

2. Tip the dough on to a lightly floured surface and form into a ball. Wrap in clingfilm and chill in the fridge for an hour.

3. Roll the dough on a lightly floured surface into a 45cm x 20cm rectangle, 1cm thick. Bash the butter with a rolling pin and flatten into a 30cm x 19cm rectangle. Place the butter on the dough so it covers the bottom two thirds.

4. Fold the dough without the butter on down so it covers one third of the butter. Cut off the exposed butter without cutting into the dough. Place this butter on top of the dough you have just folded down. Fold the bottom half of the dough up. Seal the butter in place by gently squeezing the edges. Wrap the dough in clingfilm and place in the fridge for at least an hour or until the butter has hardened.

5. Place the chilled dough, short side facing you, on a lightly floured surface. Roll into a 45cm x 20cm rectangle. Fold the bottom third of the dough up and the top third down on top, creating a single turn. Wrap the dough again and place in the fridge for an hour. Repeat this turn two more times, chilling the dough between turns. After the final turn, chill the dough for 8 hours, or overnight.

6. Make the filling by cutting the passion fruit in half and scooping out the pulp and the seeds. Place in a small processor and blitz – this makes it easier to separate the pulp and seeds. Strain, reserving the liquid and the seeds.

7. On a low heat, melt the butter in a pan. Whisk the whole eggs, yolks and sugar together. Add to the pan with the passion fruit juice. Stir constantly over a low heat until the mixture thickens and has the consistency of lemon curd. Do not be tempted to increase the heat and rush this process. It will take around

10 minutes. Remove from the heat and stir in half the passion fruit seeds and the lime juice. Tip into a bowl, cover the surface with clingfilm and leave to chill in the fridge.

8. Line three baking trays with parchment paper.

9. Take the chilled dough and cut in half. On a lightly floured surface, roll each piece into a 30cm square. Trim the edges so they are even and cut each piece of pastry into nine equal squares. On each square make 2.5cm cuts from each corner diagonally almost to the centre, so you have four triangles on each square of pastry. Fold one corner from each triangle into the centre to create a star shape.

10. Place the star-shaped pastries on the prepared trays, cover and leave to prove for 2 hours or until doubled in size.

11. Preheat your oven to 200°C/Gas 6. Make an indentation in the centre of each pastry. Fill with a teaspoon of passion fruit curd (any left over can be kept in the fridge for up to 2 weeks). Top with half an apricot, cut side down, and gently press down. Bake for 15 to 20 minutes until risen and golden. Warm the apricot glaze and mix with the remaining passion fruit seeds. Brush the pastries whilst still hot. Cool on a wire rack.

SOME OF THE BEST DANISH PASTRIES I'VE EVER TASTED

# DANISH CINNAMON SNAILS /

Makes 9

I felt a real affinity with Torben Sørensen, who runs Sankt Peder's Bageri (St Peter's Bakery), the oldest bakery in Copenhagen. Similar in age to me, he is a proud and passionate baker. He is also the keeper of the famous *onsdagssnegle*, or 'Wednesday snail', recipe. These are huge cinnamon swirls which, as the name suggests, are only available to buy in the bakery on Wednesdays. Torben will bake over a thousand pastries on a normal day (rising to 4000 on a busy day!) and his customers queue out of the door for these famous rolls. The sweet, rich, yeasted dough isn't folded many times, like a classic Danish pastry, so do have a go as they are quite straightforward to make.

**PREP:** 20 minutes

**PROVE:** 30–45 minutes

**BAKE:** 20–25 minutes

### for the dough:

500g strong white bread flour, plus extra for dusting

10g salt

10g instant yeast

60g softened unsalted butter

3 medium eggs

150ml water

### for the filling:

3 tablespoons ground cinnamon

150g softened unsalted butter

250g dark soft brown sugar

75g plain flour

150g ground almonds

### for the water icing:

200g icing sugar, sieved

2 tablespoons cold water

caster sugar, to sprinkle

1. Place the flour in a large mixing bowl, add the salt to one side and the yeast to the other side. Add the butter and the eggs and three quarters of the water. Stir together with your hands to make a rough dough. Add the remaining water if needed.

2. Tip the dough on to a lightly floured work surface and knead well for 5 minutes, until smooth and elastic. Alternatively, this can be done in a stand mixer using a dough hook.

3. Make the filling by beating all the ingredients together to form a thick paste. Line two baking trays with parchment paper.

4. Tip the dough on to a lightly floured work surface. Roll it out into a rectangle 5mm thick and tack down the long side nearest to you by pressing it down on to the work surface with your thumb. Dollop and pat the cinnamon paste over the dough using your hands. Roll the opposite long side of the dough towards you quite tightly to form a long cylinder. Trim the ends to neaten. With a sharp knife, cut the dough into nine thick rounds. Place the rounds on the prepared baking trays, quite close so they will batch together when cooked, then place each tray in a clean plastic bag and leave to prove for 30 to 45 minutes.

5. Preheat the oven to 190°C/Gas 5. When the snails have proved, bake for 20 to 25 minutes until golden brown. Remove the buns from the oven and let them cool slightly before transferring them from the trays to a cooling rack.

6. Make the water icing by stirring together the icing sugar and water and decorate the snails or just sprinkle over the caster sugar.

Egg mayonnaise / Blanched asparagus /
Cress / Extra virgin olive oil

Pickled herrings / Shallot rings / Dill

Blanched and mashed petits pois /
Cooked prawns / Chives

Pickled herrings / Beetroot / Sour cream /
Smoked mackerel / Watercress

Cream cheese / Smoked salmon / Shallots /
Capers / Chives / Black pepper

Piquillo peppers / White anchovies /
Sliced green olives

Cream cheese / Sliced radishes / Boiled
and sliced quail's eggs / Black pepper

Blanched and mashed petits pois /
Prosciutto / Pea shoots

# SEEDED RYE BREAD / Makes 1 loaf

Rye bread is a staple in Denmark due to the grain growing well in the cooler northern climate where wheat doesn't thrive. This dark dense bread is very healthy and, when sliced thinly, it's essential for making the famous Danish open sandwiches called *smørrebrød*.

**PREP:** 30 minutes

**PROVE:** 28 hours (for the starter) + 12–14 hours

**BAKE:** 55 minutes–1 hour

**for the starter:**

175g rye flour

200ml date syrup

110ml warm water

½ teaspoon instant yeast

**for the dough:**

330g rye flour

100g strong white bread flour

10g salt

1 tablespoon date syrup

375–400ml water

60g pumpkin seeds

40g linseeds

oil, for greasing

**equipment:**

2lb (900g) loaf tin

1. Mix the starter ingredients together to form a paste. Cover and leave at room temperature for 3 to 4 hours until bubbles form and it looks lively. Leave somewhere cool for at least 24 hours. If you want a very sour taste, leave the starter for 3 to 4 days before using.

2. To make the loaf, place the flours and salt in the bowl of a stand mixer. Add 100g of the starter, the date syrup and three quarters of the water. Mix slowly, adding the remaining water to form a soft, sticky dough. Mix for 5 minutes, then add the seeds and mix again until they are incorporated. Cover and leave to prove for 2 hours. The dough will be sticky and more like a cake mixture than a white bread dough.

3. Grease a 2lb (900g) loaf tin. Scrape the dough from the bowl and place in the prepared tin, levelling the top. Place the tin in a clean plastic bag and leave to prove for 10 to 12 hours in the fridge; overnight is ideal. This slow prove produces a deep flavour.

4. Preheat your oven to 170°C/Gas 3 and place an empty roasting tray in the bottom to heat up.

5. Pour hot water into the roasting tin – this will create steam and help the crust form on the loaf. The dough should have risen to the top of the tin. Place in the oven and bake for 40 minutes. After this time, remove the loaf from the tin, place the loaf directly on the shelf and bake for a further 15 to 20 minutes. Cool completely before slicing.

# CHOCOLATE AND DATE RYE BREAD LOAVES / Makes 6–8

The Danes eat a lot of rye bread; they have been baking it for generations, with the average Dane getting through about 20 to 25kg of it each year. This equates to around 8.5 to 9 million slices of various rye breads eaten in Denmark every day! So, sticking with this theme, I came up with a recipe for mini rye bread loaves. Partnering chocolate and dates with the dense richness of rye works so well.

**PREP:** 30 minutes

**PROVE:** (28 hours for the starter) + 12–14 hours

**BAKE:** 20–25 minutes

**for the starter:**

175g rye flour

200ml date syrup

110ml warm water

½ teaspoon instant yeast

**for the dough:**

60g dates, chopped

170ml water

½ teaspoon bicarbonate of soda

150g rye flour

50g strong white bread flour

50g dark soft brown sugar

5g salt

1 tablespoon date syrup

25g pumpkin seeds

25g sesame seeds

75g dark chocolate, chopped into small chunks

a few extra seeds, for sprinkling

sunflower oil, for greasing

**equipment:**

8 mini loaf tins

1. Mix the starter ingredients together to form a paste. Cover and leave at room temperature for 3 to 4 hours until bubbles form and it looks lively. Leave somewhere cool for at least 24 hours.

2. To make the loaves, heat the dates with 70ml of the water and the bicarbonate of soda. Bring to the boil, then simmer for about 10 minutes to form a paste. Remove from the heat and leave to cool.

3. In a large bowl, mix the flours, sugar and salt together. Add the date syrup, 50g of the starter, the date paste and the remaining 100ml of water. Mix well to incorporate all the ingredients and form a soft, sticky dough. Add the seeds and chopped chocolate, mixing thoroughly. Cover and leave to prove for 2 hours.

4. Grease eight mini loaf tins with a little sunflower oil and place on a baking tray. Put spoonfuls of the mixture into the prepared tins, filling almost to the top. Cover the tins with a clean plastic bag and leave to prove for 10 to 12 hours in the fridge; overnight is ideal. This slow prove produces a deep flavour.

5. Preheat your oven to 170°C/Gas 3 and place an empty roasting tray in the bottom to heat up. Pour hot water into the roasting tin – this will create steam and help the crust form on the loaves.

6. The dough should have risen to the top of the tins. Sprinkle the loaves with extra seeds, then place in the oven and bake for 20 to 25 minutes. The loaves should be risen and cooked through – check by inserting a skewer. Cool on a wire rack.

# DANISH RASPBERRY SLICES /

Makes 8

*Hindbærsnitter* are deliciously sweet Danish pastries loved by adults and children alike. Found in almost every Danish bakery, two layers of pastry are sandwiched together with a filling of raspberry jam and topped with icing. These are perfect for a children's party, and can be decorated with any kind of colourful sprinkle, although I've opted for freeze-dried raspberries to give a tart flavour to the proceedings.

**PREP:** 30 minutes

**CHILL:** 1 hour

**BAKE:** 12–15 minutes

**for the pastry:**

265g plain flour, plus extra for dusting

95g icing sugar

¼ teaspoon salt

150g unsalted butter, cut into small pieces

1 teaspoon vanilla extract

1 medium egg, beaten

**for the topping:**

175g icing sugar, sieved

1–2 tablespoons water

1 tablespoon freeze-dried raspberries

**for the filling:**

150g good-quality raspberry jam

1. Place the flour, icing sugar and salt in a bowl. Add the butter and, using your fingers, rub the butter into the mixture until it resembles fine breadcrumbs. Add the vanilla extract and egg and stir to begin to bring the ingredients together. Tip on to a lightly dusted work surface and gently knead until you have a smooth dough. Shape into a ball, wrap in clingfilm and place in the fridge for at least 30 minutes.

2. Line two baking trays with parchment paper. Dust your work surface with flour. Cut the chilled pastry in half and roll each piece into a 20cm square. Place on the prepared trays, then place in the fridge for 30 minutes to rest.

3. Preheat your oven to 200°C/Gas 6. Bake for 12 to 15 minutes until the pastry is light golden brown and cooked through. Leave to cool on a wire rack.

4. To make the topping, mix the icing sugar with half the water, adding more water until you have an icing that will spread but is not too runny. Spread the jam for the filling on to one of the pastry squares and carefully place the other pastry on top. Using a palette knife, spread the icing across the top and sprinkle with the freeze-dried raspberries. Place in the fridge to set.

5. Using a large sharp knife, trim the edges to neaten. Cut the pastry into quarters, then each quarter in half diagonally to give eight triangles.

# DANISH POPPY SEED PASTRIES / Makes 8

*Tebirkes* are classic Danish pastries found in all the bakeries in Copenhagen. Traditional Danish pastry dough is folded around a marzipan filling called *remonce* and the pastries are then topped with a thick coating of poppy seeds.

**PREP:** 1 hour

**CHILL:** 12 hours

**PROVE:** 2 hours

**BAKE:** 15–20 minutes

**for the pastry dough:**

450g strong white bread flour, plus extra for dusting

75g caster sugar

7g salt

7g instant yeast

2 medium eggs

75ml cold water

75ml full-fat milk

225g cold unsalted butter

**for the filling:**

400g almond paste (at least 50% ground almond content)

1 beaten egg, to glaze

100g black poppy seeds

1. Place the flour in the bowl of a mixer fitted with a dough hook. Put the sugar and salt at one side and the yeast at the other. Add the eggs, water and milk. Begin mixing on a slow speed for a couple of minutes to bring the ingredients together. Once combined, increase the speed and mix for 5 minutes.

2. Tip the dough on to a lightly floured surface and form into a ball. Wrap in clingfilm and chill in the fridge for an hour.

3. Roll the dough on a lightly floured surface into a 50cm x 20cm rectangle, 1cm thick. Bash the butter with a rolling pin and flatten into a 30cm x 19cm rectangle. Place the butter on the dough so it covers the bottom two thirds.

4. Fold the dough without the butter down so it covers one third of the butter. Cut off the exposed butter without cutting into the dough. Place this butter on top of the dough you have just folded down. Fold the bottom half of the dough up. Seal the butter in place by gently squeezing the edges. Wrap the dough in clingfilm and place in the fridge for at least an hour or until the butter has hardened.

5. Place the chilled dough, short side facing you, on a lightly floured surface. Roll into a 45cm x 20cm rectangle. Fold one third of the dough up and the top third down on top, creating a single turn. Wrap the dough again and place in the fridge for an hour. Repeat this turn two more times, chilling the dough between turns. After the final turn, chill the dough for 8 hours or overnight.

6. Line two baking trays with parchment paper. On a lightly floured surface, roll the almond paste into a 70cm x 10cm strip. Roll the dough into a 70cm x 30cm rectangle, 7mm thick.

7. Place the almond paste strip down the middle third of the dough. Fold the sides of the dough over the almond paste, one on top of the other, so the almond paste is wrapped in the pastry. Cut the log into eight equal pieces and place on the baking trays seam-side down. Cover and leave to rise for 2 hours.

8. Preheat your oven to 200°C/Gas 6. Once they have risen, brush the pastries with egg wash and sprinkle each pastry heavily with poppy seeds. Bake for 15 to 20 minutes until the pastry is puffed, crispy and golden. Cool on a wire rack.

# BAVARIAN BITES /

## MUNICH

Dampfnudel / Sweet and salty popcorn pretzels / Apple crumble tart /
Stollen / Lebkuchen biscuits / Prinzregententorte / Schmalznudels /
Zwiebelkuchen / Marble bundt cake

Munich is a vibrant city with so much to offer – particularly when it comes to food. It boasts a wonderful mixture of the historic and modern. Medieval architecture is found amongst new landmarks constructed from World War II ruins. It's also a major centre for art, technology and finance. So whilst it's probably best known for the hedonistic Oktoberfest, which attracts over six million visitors each year, Munich's rich cultural history and exciting food scene make it a brilliant city-break destination any time of year.

We are already familiar with some Bavarian treats, such as *Lebkuchen* and stollen (you can find my recipes for these on page 179 and page 176), but the city's bakes are varied and not just for the festival season. In Munich, baking is a highly respected career, as my friend Falko Burkert explained when I went to visit him. I had the pleasure of baking with Falko a couple of years ago and it was great to learn more about his unique style, which centres around using minimal amounts of sugar and subtle flavours. He never uses a proving machine or raising agents and the results are incredible. Falko's recipe for *Prinzregententorte* is on page 180 and I highly recommend giving it a try. Delicate layers of thin sponge interlaid with buttercream – it's quite something.

It's well worth paying a visit to Café Frischhut – a charming place with a very homely feel, found near the daily food market or *Viktualienmarkt*. The Frischhut family has been selling *Schmalznudels* since 1973; deep-fried dough rings, they are akin to a large, flat doughnut and a real favourite with the locals (my recipe is on page 185). Doused in sugar, filled with apple purée or just plain, these are absolutely delicious and the perfect partner for mid-morning coffee.

Another bake loved by the locals is the pretzel, and there's no better place to enjoy these than Hofbräuhaus. One of Munich's oldest breweries, this beer hall has been serving staple Bavarian food since 1897. Traditionally, pretzels are eaten with white sausage and sweet mustard alongside a nice cool pint, usually before midday. The technique for shaping preztels can be a bit fiddly, but the end result is really worth the effort (see page 170).

Quality of life is very high in Munich and I imagine the standard of food has something to do with this. Great care is taken in preparing and preserving their traditional bakes, and it's well worth taking some time to try these dishes at home yourself. I've provided a mix of sweet and savoury dishes – something for any occasion and for any time of the day.

# DAMPFNUDEL / Makes 6

Bavarian beer halls really are something to experience! They are huge spaces seating hundreds and sometimes thousands of drinkers. The food and drink are on a large scale: beer comes in litre glasses (no halves available) and the portions of food are huge. Staff dress in traditional costume and are on hand serving beer, pretzels and huge chunks of meat like ham hocks or meatballs with dumplings. The oompah band plays and the atmosphere is boisterous. The most traditional dessert served is the *dampfnudel*: a dumpling made from sweetened bread dough and served with vanilla custard. It's steamed, rather than baked, resulting in a cake-like texture. By themselves they are fairly plain, so the version I'm giving you here is stuffed with cherries. A stewed apple filling would be equally delicious.

**PREP:** 40 minutes

**PROVE:** 1–3 hours

**BAKE:** 20–25 minutes

### for the dough:

220ml full-fat milk

50g softened unsalted butter

450g strong white bread flour,
   plus extra for dusting

7g instant yeast

60g caster sugar

1 teaspoon salt

1 medium egg

1. Place the milk and butter for the dough in a small pan and heat gently so the butter melts and the milk is warm.

2. For the filling, drain the cherries over a bowl so you catch all the syrup, then heat the syrup in a pan with the caster sugar. Mix the cornflour with a little cold water to slacken, then add to the warm syrup in the pan. Heat until it begins to boil and thicken. Remove from the heat and add the drained cherries.

3. Place the flour for the dough in a large bowl, add the yeast to one side and the sugar and salt to the other. Crack the egg into the middle and gradually add the warm milk and butter (make sure the milk is warm and not hot). Using your hand, bring the mixture together until a soft dough is formed. Place on a lightly floured work surface and knead for 5 minutes until you have a smooth dough. Place in a lightly greased bowl, cover and leave to prove until doubled in size. This will take between 1 and 3 hours.

**for the filling:**

425g tin or jar of pitted
  cherries in light syrup
  (350g net weight)

2 tablespoons caster sugar

20g cornflour

**for the cooking liquid:**

50g unsalted butter

1 teaspoon salt

2 tablespoons caster sugar

water

**for the custard:**

1 vanilla pod

500ml full-fat milk

6 egg yolks

100g caster sugar

1 tablespoon cornflour

icing sugar, to dust

4. Tip the dough on to a lightly floured surface and divide into six
   equal pieces. Place three or four cherries in the middle of each
   ball and bring the dough up around them; pinch the top to seal.
   Turn each ball over and place with the pinched side down on
   a work surface. Gently roll each one into a ball. Place on a tray
   and leave to prove for 10 minutes.

5. Gently heat a large casserole pan (approx. 28cm). Add the
   butter for the cooking liquid so it begins to melt, then add
   the salt and sugar and stir. Take the dumplings and begin by
   placing one in the centre of the pan, then place the remaining
   ones around the edge, leaving space between them to expand.
   Pour in enough water so there is about 2cm in the base of the
   pan. Cover and cook on a low to medium heat for 15 to 20
   minutes. After this time, remove the lid. If there is still liquid
   present, increase the heat and cook for a further 5 minutes. Be
   careful not to burn the base – the dumplings should be golden
   on the bottom, set on the top and doubled in size.

6. Whilst they are cooking, make the custard. Split the vanilla pod
   in half and scrape out the seeds. Place the seeds in a pan with
   the milk. Heat to just below boiling point. In a bowl, beat the
   egg yolks, sugar and cornflour until well mixed. Pour the hot
   milk on to the egg yolk mixture and whisk continuously, return
   to the pan and simmer on a very low heat until the custard has
   thickened. Don't rush this and increase the heat or the custard
   will split.

7. To serve, remove the dumplings from the pan, dust with icing
   sugar and pour over the custard. You can serve any remaining
   cherries on the side.

# SWEET AND SALTY POPCORN PRETZELS /

Makes 10

Giant pretzels are sold to accompany the beer in Munich, but smaller versions are also available for those with smaller appetites. Here is my twist with a topping of crushed salty and sweet popcorn. Sounds a bit odd, but it works very well.

**PREP:** 40 minutes

**PROVE:** 1 hour

**FREEZE:** 1 hour

**BAKE:** 12–15 minutes

**for the dough:**

450g strong white bread flour

7g salt

7g instant yeast

30g softened unsalted butter

1 tablespoon malt extract

250ml full-fat milk

20g bicarbonate of soda

**to finish:**

20g sweet popcorn, crushed

20g salty popcorn, crushed

1. Line two baking trays with parchment paper.

2. Place the flour in a bowl with the salt on one side and the yeast on the other. Add the softened butter. Dissolve the malt extract in the milk by gently heating until just warm (do not boil or it will kill the yeast). Slowly add the milk mixture to the flour and mix to bring all the ingredients together until a soft dough is formed. It should be a little sticky.

3. Place the dough on a clean work surface and knead until smooth and shiny; this will take about 10 minutes.

4. Divide the dough into 10 equal pieces and roll them into long ropes. Each piece should be about 50–60cm in length. As you roll out the ropes, you should apply pressure to the dough, working from the middle outwards and using the heel of your hands. Taper the ends so they are thinner than the middle.

5. The traditional way to shape pretzels is to take hold of each end of the strand and lift it into the air to create a U-shape. Then, without letting go of the ends, and in one swift movement, flip the centre of the U, propelling it to form a double twist. Lay it back down on the work surface and lightly press the tapered ends on to the opposite sides of the pretzel, attaching them either side of the central bulge. You may find a little dab of water helps to stick the ends to the pretzel. Carefully flip the pretzels over and on to the baking trays so that the ends are face down. You should now have a classic pretzel shape with three equally spaced sections.

6. Place the pretzels on the trays in clean plastic bags and leave to prove for about an hour. Once risen, place in the freezer for at least an hour.

7. Preheat the oven to 200°C/Gas 6.

8. Add the bicarbonate of soda to a wide-based pan of boiling water, and gently drop each pretzel into the boiling water for approximately 10 seconds. Gently remove and place on a baking tray. With a sharp knife, make a deep slash into the thickest part of the dough. Sprinkle with the crushed popcorn – it will stick to the surface as it's wet. Bake in the oven for 12 to 15 minutes, or until the pretzels are a deep golden brown colour. Cool on a wire rack.

# APPLE CRUMBLE TART / Serves 12

Crisp, buttery, sweet shortcrust pastry, sharp apple filling and lots of crumbly topping – these are the ingredients for a perfect apple crumble tart. My crumble recipe is slightly different to the more usual ones, as I use melted butter instead of rubbing in diced cold butter. The result is a lovely uneven crumble, which adds texture to the tart and a rustic, homemade finish. What more could you want?

**PREP:** 1 hour

**CHILL:** 45 minutes

**BAKE:** 20–25 minutes

**for the pastry:**

200g plain flour, plus extra for dusting

2 tablespoons icing sugar

100g cold unsalted butter, diced

1 medium egg, beaten

½ a teaspoon lemon juice

2 teaspoons very cold water

**for the filling:**

4 large Bramley apples (about 1.2kg), peeled, cored and cut into chunks

140g caster sugar

1 tablespoon water

**for the crumble topping:**

275g plain flour

100g rolled oats

125g light soft brown sugar

225g melted unsalted butter

2 tablespoons semolina

double cream or custard, to serve

**equipment:**

25cm loose bottom tart tin

1.  To make the pastry, mix the flour and icing sugar together in a bowl. Add the diced butter and rub it in with your fingertips until the mixture looks like fine breadcrumbs. Mix the egg with the lemon juice and water. Make a well in the centre of the flour mixture and pour in the egg mix. Using one hand, work the liquid into the flour to bring the pastry together. If it's a little too dry, add a splash more water. When the dough begins to stick together, gently knead into a ball. Wrap in clingfilm and leave to rest in the fridge for 30 minutes.

2.  Place the dough on a lightly floured work surface and roll it out into a circle about 3mm thick. Press the pastry into the base and sides of a 25cm loose bottom tart tin and leave the excess pastry hanging over the edge. Prick the base all over with a fork, then chill in the fridge for 15 minutes.

3.  Preheat the oven to 200°C/Gas 6. Line the chilled pastry case with parchment paper and baking beans.

4.  Bake the pastry case in the oven for 12 to 15 minutes, or until the edges are light golden brown. Remove the baking beans and paper, and bake for a further 5 to 8 minutes, or until the pastry case is crisp and golden brown all over. Once cooled, carefully trim the edges to neaten and remove any overhanging pastry.

5.  For the filling, place the apples, caster sugar and water in a large, deep saucepan and cook over a medium heat for 5 minutes, stirring occasionally. Cover the pan with the lid and bring the mixture to a gentle simmer. Cook gently until the apple has softened but not collapsed. Set aside to cool.

6.  To make the crumble, mix the flour, oats and brown sugar together in a large bowl, then stir in the melted butter until the mixture forms large crumbs.

7.  Sprinkle the semolina across the base of the cooked tart – this helps to mop up any juice from the apple and prevents the base going soggy. Spread the cooled apple filling into the case. Sprinkle the crumble topping all over the apple filling and bake the tart at 200°C/Gas 6 for 20 to 25 minutes, or until the crumble is crisp and golden brown.

8.  Serve the tart warm, in slices, with double cream or custard.

# STOLLEN / Serves 10

Stollen is a traditional German fruit bread packed with dried or candied fruit, nuts and spices and often covered in icing sugar. It's usually eaten at Christmas and is a rich, sweet treat. The strip of marzipan in the middle is optional, but I like to include it for extra flavour and a different texture. Leave it out if you're not a fan. Why not try making this as well as, or instead of, Christmas cake next year?

**PREP:** 20 minutes

**PROVE:** 2–4 hours

**BAKE:** 1 hour

450g strong white bread flour, plus extra for dusting

90g caster sugar

7g instant yeast

7g salt

125g softened unsalted butter, plus extra for greasing

225ml full-fat milk

½ teaspoon ground cinnamon

¼ teaspoon freshly grated nutmeg

zest of 1 orange

100g raisins

100g sultanas

75g dried cranberries

100g mixed peel

50g chopped almonds

20g melted unsalted butter

200g marzipan

**to serve:**

2 tablespoons melted unsalted butter

icing sugar, for dusting

1. Place the flour and caster sugar in a large bowl. Add the yeast to one side of the bowl and salt to the other. Add the butter and three quarters of the milk. Turn the mixture around with your fingers. Continue to add the remaining milk, a little at a time, until all the flour is incorporated.

2. Tip the dough on to a lightly floured surface and knead for 5 to 10 minutes until you have a soft, smooth dough. Place in a lightly greased bowl, cover and leave to prove for 1 to 3 hours until doubled in size.

3. In a large bowl, mix the cinnamon, nutmeg and orange zest with all the dried fruit and chopped almonds.

4. Line a large baking tray with parchment paper.

5. Tip the risen dough on to a lightly floured surface and knock back. Shape into a large rectangle. Scatter the dried fruit mixture over the dough. Fold the dough over the fruit, then knead until the fruit is evenly mixed in.

6. Dust the work surface again with flour and roll out the dough to 40cm x 30cm. Brush with melted butter.

7. Roll the marzipan into a long strip approximately 30cm x 15cm. Place the marzipan strip in the centre of the dough. Roll the dough around the marzipan so the seam runs along the bottom and place on the prepared tray. Place the tray in a clean plastic bag and leave to prove for about an hour or until the stollen has doubled in size.

8. Preheat your oven to 190°C/Gas 5. Bake for an hour until the stollen has risen and is golden brown. If it browns too quickly, place some foil over the top. Brush with melted butter whilst still warm (this helps keep it moist) and dust heavily with icing sugar. Cool on a wire rack.

# LEBKUCHEN BISCUITS / Makes 20

These soft-style gingerbread biscuits are German Yuletide treats and very simple to make. The combination of spices gives a real Christmassy feel.

**PREP:** 30 minutes

**CHILL:** 4 hours

**BAKE:** 15 minutes

100g softened unsalted butter

100g caster sugar

100g dark soft brown sugar

3 large eggs

350g plain flour, plus extra for dusting

1 teaspoon baking powder

125g ground almonds

2 tablespoons cocoa powder

1 teaspoon ground cinnamon

1 teaspoon ground ginger

¼ teaspoon ground cloves

¼ teaspoon ground allspice

¼ teaspoon ground nutmeg

¼ teaspoon ground cardamom

a splash of full-fat milk

**for the icing:**

200g icing sugar

2 tablespoons water

**equipment:**

cookie cutter

1. Cream the butter and sugars together until the sugars have dissolved and the mix is light and fluffy. Add the eggs, one at a time, and beat after each addition. Fold in the dry ingredients, then add enough milk to bring all the ingredients together and form a soft dough – you may not need any milk. Cover and chill for at least 4 hours.

2. Preheat your oven to 180°C/Gas 4 and line two baking trays with parchment paper.

3. On a floured work surface, roll out half the dough to 5mm thick. Using a cutter of your choice, stamp out shapes and place on the prepared tray, allowing room to spread. Repeat using the remaining dough.

4. Bake for 15 minutes. The biscuits will have risen and be golden brown on the surface. Transfer to a wire rack to cool.

5. To make the icing, mix the icing sugar with the water to form a smooth icing. Spread or pipe the icing over the surface of the biscuits. Leave to set before eating.

# PRINZREGENTENTORTE /

Serves 16

Falko Burkert is a German *Konditormeister* – a highly skilled baker who has spent years perfecting his craft. Only *Konditormeisters* are allowed to make certain cakes like the traditional *Baumkuchen*, which is a cake baked on a spit (see photos on page 182). Falko was the perfect guide to show me around Munich. We talked about the *Prinzregententorte*, which is named after the Bavarian Prince Regent Luitpold, who began his reign in 1886. It is made up of sponge layers which signify the regions of Bavaria during his reign – I love it when food is tied to a place for geographic or historic reasons! Every layer has to be the same so it's all about precision, perfection and accuracy. Falko now lives in Edinburgh, where you can find his Falko bakeries, and the recipe below is from him. He tempers the chocolate covering to give it a glossy finish but this is quite an elaborate process so feel free to simply melt it, which is what I tend to do.

**PREP:** 1¼ hours

**BAKE:** 12–15 minutes

**CHILL:** 3 hours

**for the sponges:**

300g unsalted butter,
  at room temperature

300g caster sugar

9 egg yolks, at room
  temperature

14 egg whites

300g plain flour

1. Preheat the oven to 200°C/Gas 6.

2. First make the sponges. Using an electric whisk, cream the butter and the 75g of the sugar together until the sugar has dissolved. Add each egg yolk one at a time and mix well after each addition. The mixture will turn pale and fluffy.

3. In a separate bowl, whisk the egg whites until stiff. A spoonful at a time, add the remaining 225g of sugar and whisk to form stiff peaks.

4. Add one third of the egg whites to the butter and egg yolk mix and stir until smooth. Add the remaining whites and fold in gently until the mixture is smooth. Sieve the flour over the mixture and fold gently until smooth.

5. Using a palette knife, spread the mix out evenly between seven pieces of parchment paper, forming circles slightly larger than 26cm. Make sure they are of even height and don't overwork the mix.

6. Bake for approximately 12 to 15 minutes until the sponge bounces back when you press your finger on the top. Take out immediately and cool on wire racks.

## for the chocolate buttercream:

500ml milk

1 vanilla pod

3 egg yolks

250g caster sugar

50g cornflour

50g cocoa power

100g dark chocolate (minimum 60% cocoa solids)

500g softened unsalted butter

## for the covering:

1kg dark chocolate (minimum 60% cocoa solids), tempered

## equipment:

metal 26cm disc (the base of a cake tin works well) and ring

7. To make the chocolate buttercream, pour the milk into a pan and scrape the vanilla seeds from the pod and add to the milk. Bring the milk just to the boil then remove from the heat.

8. Whisk the egg yolks with the sugar, cornflour and cocoa powder. Pour the hot milk on to the egg yolk mixture and whisk. Return to the pan and stir over a gentle heat until the mixture thickens. Pour into a bowl, cover the surface with clingfilm and leave to cool.

9. Melt the chocolate in a small bowl set over, but not touching, a pan of simmering water. Leave to cool.

10. Whisk the butter until pale and fluffy. Slowly mix in the cooled custard until thoroughly combined. Add the melted chocolate and whisk again until thoroughly combined.

11. Turn the sponge discs upside down and remove the baking parchment. Using a metal 26cm ring, trim the sponges to form seven even circles.

12. Place a sponge circle on a metal disc, then put the ring around it. Place approximately 200g of the chocolate buttercream on the sponge and spread evenly. Place the next sponge on top and repeat. Continue layering the rest of the sponges on top.

13. Allow the cake to rest in a fridge for at least 2 hours to set the buttercream. Keep the remaining buttercream at room temperature.

14. Remove the metal ring from around the cake. A quick blast with a blow torch will help, or wrap with a hot clean cloth. Spread the remaining buttercream over the top and sides until you have a perfect smooth surface. Place the cake in the fridge to firm up for at least an hour.

15. Temper the 1kg of chocolate and cover the cake with it.

16. Let the chocolate set, then divide the cake into 16 portions, using a hot dry knife.

# SCHMALZNUDELS / Makes 10

Café Frischhut in Munich is unique: it serves only tea, coffee and four types of *Schmalznudels* (doughnuts). The fryers are switched on first thing and by midday customers are forming large queues. These Bavarian treats are not coated in icing or highly decorated; instead, they are simple, yeasted batter creations – some round, others twisted. The recipe I'm giving you here is for flat round ones that have a thick crust. Simple and delicious!

**PREP:** 30 minutes

**PROVE:** 1–3 hours

**FRY:** 3–4 minutes per doughnut

220–240ml full-fat milk

60g softened unsalted butter, plus extra for greasing

500g strong white bread flour, plus extra for dusting

10g instant yeast

75g caster sugar, plus extra for sprinkling

a pinch of salt

1 large egg

sunflower oil, for frying

1. Place the milk and butter in a small pan and heat gently so the butter melts and the milk is warm.

2. Place the flour in a large bowl, add the yeast to one side and the sugar and salt to the other. Crack the egg into the middle and gradually add three quarters of the milk and butter (make sure the milk is warm and not hot). Using your hand, bring the mixture together until a soft dough is formed. Add more milk if the dough is too dry. Turn out on a lightly floured work surface and knead for 5 minutes until you have a smooth dough. Place in a lightly greased bowl, cover and leave to prove for 1 to 3 hours until doubled in size.

3. Tip the dough on to a lightly floured surface and divide into 10 equal pieces. Flatten each piece into a disc shape, then pull from the middle outwards, giving you a thin centre and a thicker outer crust.

4. Heat a deep-fat fryer or three quarters fill a large wide pan or wok with sunflower oil. Place the doughnuts in the hot oil, one at a time, and fry until golden and puffed. Turn over and cook the other side. Drain on kitchen paper and sprinkle with extra sugar.

# ZWIEBELKUCHEN / Serves 6

*Zwiebelkuchen* is a German onion cake, which I just had to include. The sweet smell of onions cooking filled one of the bakeries I was visiting in Munich, which was unusual as most bakeries have a sweet sugary or bread aroma. I enquired what they were making and it was onion cake. It's not technically a cake, though, more a quiche made with a yeast dough as the crust. Here's my version for you. Sweet caramelised onions, a little bacon, eggs, cream and caraway – what's not to like?

**PREP:** 40 minutes

**PROVE:** 1 hour

**BAKE:** 35–40 minutes

**for the pastry:**

350g strong white bread flour

7g instant yeast

½ teaspoon salt

1 medium egg

75g softened unsalted butter

125–150ml warm full-fat milk

olive oil, for greasing

**for the filling:**

75g unsalted butter

1 tablespoon sunflower oil

4 large onions, peeled and finely chopped

200g plain back bacon, cut into small dice

½ teaspoon caraway seeds

4 medium eggs

2 egg yolks

100ml double cream

100ml soured cream

a pinch of salt and a little ground white pepper

lard, for greasing

**equipment:**

23cm x 7cm deep spring form cake tin

1. Place the flour in a large mixing bowl. Add the yeast to one side and the salt to the other. Add the egg, butter and three quarters of the warm milk. Use your hand to bring all the ingredients together. Gradually add the remaining milk to form a dough. Tip the dough on to a lightly floured surface and knead for 5 to 10 minutes until smooth. Place into a lightly oiled bowl, cover and leave to prove for about an hour.

2. To make the filling, melt the butter and oil in a large wide-based pan, add the onions and stir so they are coated in the butter. Cut a circle of baking paper the same size as the pan, wet the paper and screw it up, then flatten out and place on the onions (this helps to stop them catching as they cook). Very gently cook the onions, stirring every now and again, until they are soft and turn a golden caramel colour. Be patient, this takes a long time. Remove from the pan and leave to one side.

3. In the same pan, increase the heat to medium and add the bacon and caraway seeds. Cook until the bacon is just turning crispy round the edges. Add the bacon to the bowl with the onions and leave to cool.

4. Preheat your oven to 200°C/Gas 6. Grease a 23cm x 7cm deep spring form cake tin with lard.

5. Tip the dough on to a lightly floured surface and roll into a large circle 7mm thick. Line the prepared tin with the dough and trim the edge to neaten.

6. Beat the eggs and egg yolks with the double and soured cream and season with a pinch of salt and a little white pepper. Add the onions, bacon and caraway and stir. Pour into the lined tin. Don't worry if there doesn't seem to be enough filling: the dough will shrink and the filling will rise.

7. Bake for 15 minutes, then lower the heat to 180°C/Gas 4 and bake for a further 25 to 30 minutes until the crust is crisp and the filling is set and golden. Leave to cool in the tin for 15 minutes. Serve warm or cold.

# MARBLE BUNDT CAKE / Serves 12

This cake is named after the shape of the bundt tin that it is made in. Originally thought to have been based on a European style of cake, it also became hugely popular in America in the fifties and sixties. This recipe makes a lot of cake mix and it's therefore easier to make it using a stand mixer. The alternative is to halve the quantities and make two mixes using an electric hand whisk.

**PREP:** 20 minutes

**BAKE:** 1½ hours

475g softened unsalted butter, plus extra for greasing

475g self-raising flour, plus extra for dusting

475g caster sugar

4 medium eggs

1 teaspoon baking powder

2 teaspoons vanilla extract

3 tablespoons cocoa powder

**for the chocolate ganache:**

115g dark chocolate

60g double cream

25g unsalted butter

**equipment:**

2 litre bundt tin

1. Preheat the oven to 150°C/Gas 2. Grease a 2 litre bundt tin with butter and dust with flour.

2. Place the butter and sugar in the bowl of a stand mixer fitted with the whisk attachment and beat together until light and fluffy. Add the eggs one at a time and beat well after each addition.

3. Mix together the baking powder and flour. Add to the butter, sugar and egg mix along with the vanilla extract. Whisk on a slow speed for 2 minutes until all the ingredients are combined. You may have to use a spatula and scrape down the sides of the bowl, then mix again.

4. Spoon half the cake mix into a separate bowl. Fold the cocoa powder into one half of the mixture. Add spoonfuls of each mixture alternately to the prepared tin, then drag a skewer through the mixture to create a marbled swirl effect.

5. Bake the cake for 1½ hours until it is well risen. To check, insert a skewer into the deepest part of the cake – it should come out clean. Let the cake cool in the tin for 10 minutes before turning out on to a wire rack.

6. For the chocolate ganache, place the chocolate, cream and butter in a bowl and sit this over a pan of simmering water. Stir occasionally until you have a melted, smooth glossy sauce. Leave to cool slightly before using. Place a tray under the wire rack and pour the chocolate ganache over the cake. Allow the chocolate to set before slicing.

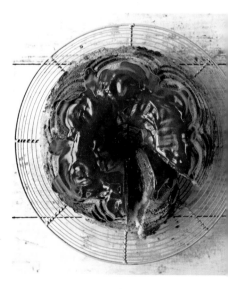

# AMERICAN PIE /

## NEW YORK

Bagels / Kale, cherry and cheese scones / Brioche ring doughnuts /
No-knead bread / Breakfast buns with bacon and cheese /
New York-style baked cheesecake / Chocolate cheesecake brownies

With more restaurants, bars, theatres, galleries and iconic sights than you can imagine, New York is an unbelievably exciting city. It's hard to know where to start, but it's certainly not hard to find something delicious to eat. New York is well known for the quality of its food, but also for its diversity – delicacies from hundreds of different countries can all be found within a few city blocks.

You can't possibly visit New York without having a bagel and I went to Sadelle's to try this classic bake. Located on West Broadway, Sadelle's was the most hotly anticipated restaurant launch of 2015 and co-owner Melissa Weller showed me exactly why. Featuring a stunning glass-walled bakery right in the centre of the dining area, you can see the bagels being expertly rolled and shaped until the seam of the dough nearly disappears. It's also worth heading to Greenwich Village to Murray's Bagels, where customers queue out the door at weekends. To try this traditional New York breakfast treat at home, see my recipe on page 196.

From century-old bakes like the bagel, to something new that is taking the city by storm – the cronut. The cronut was invented in the Dominique Ansel Bakery in 2013 and owner Ansel showed me why customers queue for up to 2 hours to try it. This croissant-doughnut hybrid is such a simple concept, but really delivers on flavour and texture. If you're after something slightly more conventional, try my own doughnut recipe on page 204.

Indulging comes easily whilst you're in this city and there's nothing more indulgent than a traditional New York cheesecake. Junior's in Brooklyn is a family-owned bakery and I met with the founder's grandson, Alan Rosen, to learn more about their award-winning recipe. Alan believes in using only premium ingredients, from the cream cheese to the fresh double cream – no additives, no fillers and no water. The end result is a rich, smooth consistency, something I've recreated on page 215 with my New York-style baked cheesecake. In the spirit of New York hybrid baking, I've also provided a recipe for chocolate cheesecake brownies on page 216.

From its fine-dining restaurants to the thousands of street vendors, New York's cuisine is diverse and constantly evolving. Ask locals where to find the best traditional bakes and keep your eye out for exciting new ones. The recipes I've provided here give only a slim insight into New York's vast culinary offering – a little taste of this amazing city to share with your friends and family.

# BAGELS / Makes 10

Jewish immigrants brought the bagel to the USA in the 1880s when they settled on Manhattan's Lower East Side and opened thriving bakeries. Today, classic New York delis all offer a huge variety of bagels made from many different flours: plain, wholemeal and rye. These are flavoured with an assortment of ingredients including poppy, caraway and sesame seeds, garlic, onion and salt. Or sweet flavours like blueberry and chocolate. The bagel is then filled with any choice of filling you can imagine; for me, you can't beat the classic combination of soft cream cheese with smoked salmon.

**PREP:** 35 minutes

**PROVE:** 1½–3½ hours

**BAKING:** 25–30 minutes

500g strong white bread flour, plus extra for dusting

7g instant yeast

1 tablespoon dark soft brown sugar

7g salt

320ml water

oil, for greasing

2 tablespoons molasses

1 teaspoon bicarbonate of soda

**for the topping:**

poppy, pumpkin, sesame, caraway or fennel seeds, to sprinkle

optional: sea salt, to sprinkle

1. Place the flour in a mixing bowl, add the yeast to one side and the sugar and salt to the other side. Add three quarters of the water and turn the mixture around with your fingers. Continue to add the remaining water, a little at a time, until all the flour is incorporated and you have a rough dough. You may not need all the water.

2. Tip the dough on to a lightly floured surface and knead for 5 to 10 minutes until you have a soft, smooth dough. Place in a lightly greased bowl, cover and leave to prove for 1 to 3 hours or until doubled in size.

3. Line two baking trays with parchment paper. Remove the dough from the bowl and divide into 10 equal pieces, weighing about 80g each. Roll each piece into a ball. With your finger, poke a hole through the centre of each ball and slowly ease the hole wider. Place these on the prepared trays. Cover and leave to prove for a further 30 minutes.

4. Preheat your oven to 200°C/Gas 6. Bring a large saucepan of water to the boil. Add the molasses (this will add a sweetness to the bagels) and the bicarbonate of soda (this helps to form the shine and the chewy texture of the crust) to the water.

5. Plunge the bagels, two at a time or more depending on the size of your pan, into the boiling water. Cook for 30 seconds, then turn over and cook the other side. The bagels should puff and the circular shape should set. Use a slotted spoon to remove and place back on the trays.

6. Sprinkle the top of the bagels with your chosen topping. Bake for 20 to 25 minutes until the bagels are golden brown and cooked through. Cool on a wire rack.

# KALE, CHERRY AND CHEESE SCONES / Makes 10

New York is such an exciting place for food discoveries. I spent a leisurely hour or so at the Union Square farmers' market, which I encourage you to visit if you ever find yourself looking for things to do in this amazing city. It was in the run-up to Christmas and I chatted to farmers and local food producers, whilst having a taste of their wares. I came across a baking stall that sold incredible flavours of scones, including a kale and cranberry version – bang on trend (kale) and totally Christmassy (cranberries). I had to produce my own recipe, in which I've chosen to use dried cherries instead of cranberries.

**PREP:** 20 minutes

**BAKE:** 20–25 minutes

75g kale, thick stalks removed

380g plain flour, plus extra for dusting

1 teaspoon baking powder

½ teaspoon bicarbonate of soda

¼ teaspoon salt

a pinch of ground white pepper

190g cold unsalted butter, cut into small pieces

60g dried cherries

75g mature Cheddar, grated

1 medium egg, beaten

150–180ml buttermilk

1 beaten egg, to glaze

**equipment:**

6.5cm round cutter

1. Place the kale leaves in a steamer and cook for 2 to 3 minutes or until the kale has softened. Drain on kitchen paper and leave to cool. Roughly chop so all the pieces are similar sizes.

2. Line a baking tray with parchment paper and preheat your oven to 200°C/Gas 6.

3. Place the flour, baking powder, bicarbonate of soda, salt and pepper in a mixing bowl. Add the butter and, using your fingers, rub into the flour until it resembles fine breadcrumbs. Add the cherries, chopped kale and grated cheese and mix well. Add 1 beaten egg and half the buttermilk. Stir to begin to bring the ingredients together. Add enough of the remaining buttermilk to form a soft dough. Try not to overwork the dough.

4. Tip on to a lightly floured surface and lightly press down. Fold the dough in half, turn 90 degrees and fold again. Repeat this a few times until you have a smooth dough. If the mixture becomes sticky, add a little more flour. By folding and turning you add air to the mixture, but be careful not to overwork the dough.

5. Sprinkle the surface with a little more flour. Roll the dough to 2.5cm thick. Using a 6.5cm cutter, stamp out rounds and place on the baking tray. Brush the tops with egg wash and bake for 20 to 25 minutes until risen and golden brown.

6. Leave the scones to cool on a wire rack. Serve with butter or cream cheese.

7. Store any left over in Tupperware for up to 4 days and reheat in the oven.

# BRIOCHE RING DOUGHNUTS / Makes 10

Fany Gerson, the owner of Dough Doughnuts in New York, is a Mexican pastry chef who takes doughnuts to another level. They are brioche-based, light and fluffy, made with love and care. Dough has become a destination bakery, with customers coming in all day long for boxes of doughnuts. Fany draws inspiration from everything she sees around her, from art galleries to the melting pot of cultures that make up New York. She currently offers nine different flavours every day, as well as seasonal specials such as margarita in summer and stout and chocolate in winter. Here is my version of a brioche ring doughnut, inspired by those I tasted in Dough.

**PREP:** 1 hour

**PROVE:** 8 hours or overnight + 1 hour

**FRYING:** 3–4 minutes per doughnut

225g strong white bread flour, plus extra for dusting

30g milk powder

25g caster sugar

½ teaspoon salt

1 teaspoon instant yeast

1 teaspoon freshly grated nutmeg

70ml warm full-fat milk

2 medium eggs

100g softened unsalted butter, plus extra for greasing

sunflower oil, for frying

1. To make the dough, put the flour, milk powder and sugar into the bowl of a mixer fitted with a dough hook and add the salt to one side and the yeast to the other. Add the nutmeg, milk and the eggs and mix for about 5 minutes until smooth.

2. Knead the dough on a slow speed for 5 minutes, then gradually start to add the butter. Once all the butter has been incorporated and the dough is smooth and sticky, increase the speed and knead for a further 6 minutes. Scrape the dough into a large greased bowl, cover with clingfilm and place in the fridge for 8 hours or overnight.

3. Line two baking trays with parchment paper.

4. Lightly dust the work surface with flour, turn out the dough and knock it back. Roll the dough to 1.5cm thick and cut out rounds using a 7.5cm cutter. Cut out the middle of each doughnut with a 3.5cm cutter. Place the doughnuts on the prepared trays and cover with a clean plastic bag. Leave to prove for an hour or until doubled in size.

5. Heat a deep-fat fryer to 180°C or three quarters fill a large wide pan or wok with the sunflower oil. Gently place the doughnuts, two at a time, in the pan or the fryer. They will puff up and float, so you will need to turn them over periodically so that they cook evenly on all sides. They do take on colour quickly because of the sugar and butter in the dough, but you need to cook them for about 3 to 4 minutes so that they cook through.

*Choice of toppings
(each makes enough
for 10 doughnuts)*

**for lemon and poppy seed
icing:**

200g icing sugar, sifted

2 tablespoons lemon juice

zest of 1 lemon

2 tablespoons poppy seeds

**for toffee apple crumble
topping:**

40g unsalted butter

75g plain flour

40g demerara sugar

1 teaspoon ground cinnamon

1 x 450g jar of caramel or
dulce de leche

50g dried apple rings,
cut into tiny pieces

**equipment:**

7.5cm and 3.5cm cutters

6. Remove the doughnuts from the fryer using a slotted spoon and drain them on kitchen paper. Finish with a topping of your choice.

7. To make the lemon and poppy seed icing, simply mix the icing sugar with the lemon juice and zest. Whilst the doughnuts are still warm (this gives a thin glaze), dip the top in the icing, sprinkle with poppy seeds and leave to cool.

8. For the toffee apple crumble topping, preheat your oven to 190°C/Gas 5. Rub the butter into the flour until the mixture resembles breadcrumbs, then stir in the demerara sugar and cinnamon. Tip on to a baking tray and bake for 15 minutes until golden brown. Leave to cool.

9. Tip the caramel into a bowl and beat with a wooden spoon until smooth. Take the cooled doughnuts and dip into the caramel, coating the top. Sprinkle with the chopped dried apple and the crumble.

THE MEETING OF MINDS; JIM LAHEY'S IDEAS ARE AMAZING. MY BROTHER FROM ANOTHER MOTHER

# NO-KNEAD BREAD / Makes 1 round loaf

Jim Lahey opened the Sullivan Street Bakery in 1994 and introduced New Yorkers to new styles of bread. He is a maverick baker, producing an incredible range of breads with different textures and flavours. His passion and understanding of the ingredients is second to none and I got to see him at work and learn his famous no-knead bread technique. Jim developed a way to bake bread without much intervention; he simply mixes the ingredients together then leaves the dough to ferment. This allows the deep flavours to develop. The dough is then baked in a large casserole pot with a lid and the resulting loaf has a rich, deep chestnut colour, a thick crispy crust and an airy crumb with an incredible flavour.

**PREP:** 15 minutes

**PROVE:** 13–20 hours

**BAKE:** 45 minutes–1 hour

400g strong white bread flour, plus extra for dusting

8g salt

1g instant yeast

300ml cool water

wheat bran, semolina or extra flour, for dusting

1. In a large bowl, stir together the flour, salt and yeast. Add the water and, using a wooden spoon or your hand, mix until you have a wet, sticky dough. This will take about 30 seconds. It should be very sticky to the touch; if not, add 1 to 2 tablespoons more water. Cover the bowl with clingfilm and leave at room temperature but out of direct sunlight for 12 to 18 hours until the dough has more than doubled in size and the surface is scattered with bubbles.

2. Once the dough has risen, generously dust your work surface with flour. Scrape the dough out of the bowl in one piece using a plastic scraper. As you pull the dough away from the edge of the bowl, it will cling in long thin strands. It will be quite loose and sticky but don't be tempted to add more flour.

3. Dust your hands with flour and lift the edges of the dough in towards the centre. Tuck the edges in to form a round shape.

4. Take a clean cotton or linen tea towel and place it on your work surface. Generously dust the cloth with wheat bran, semolina or flour. Use your hands to gently lift the dough in one movement on to the cloth with the seam sitting on the cloth. Dust the top with wheat bran, semolina or flour. Fold the ends of the towel loosely over the dough to cover it and leave in a warm, draught-free space to rise for 1 to 2 hours. The dough is ready when it has almost doubled in size. If you press gently with your finger, making an indentation 7mm deep, it should hold the impression. If it doesn't, leave for another 15 minutes.

5. Preheat your oven to 240°C/Gas 9 and place a large casserole dish with a lid on the bottom shelf. Heat for 30 minutes.

6. Using oven gloves, carefully remove the hot casserole dish and lift off the lid. Unfold the tea towel and lightly dust the dough with extra flour or bran. Lift the dough with the cloth or your hands and invert it into the hot casserole dish. Place the lid back on the casserole dish and bake for 30 minutes.

7. Remove the lid and continue to bake for 15 to 30 minutes until the crust is a deep chestnut colour. Remove the casserole from the oven. Carefully take out the bread and cool completely on a wire rack for at least an hour. Don't be tempted to cut or tear the bread until it has cooled completely.

# BREAKFAST BUNS WITH BACON AND CHEESE / Makes 8

This is a recipe for a lightly enriched dough made into individual rolls. Using less butter and eggs than a typical brioche, it still delivers a light texture. They are delicious with melted cheese and bacon and that's how I ate them in New York for breakfast. I enjoyed them so much I ordered seconds!

**PREP:** 25 minutes

**PROVE:** 7–9 hours

**BAKE:** 20–25 minutes

450g strong white bread flour, plus extra for dusting

7g salt

40g caster sugar

10g instant yeast

50ml lukewarm full-fat milk

1 large egg

175–200ml water

50g softened unsalted butter

**to serve:**

220g cooked bacon

200g Gruyère cheese, grated

1. Put the flour into the bowl of a mixer fitted with a dough hook. Add the salt and sugar to one side of the bowl and the yeast to the other.

2. Add the milk, egg and half the water and mix on a slow speed for 2 minutes to bring the ingredients together. Gradually add enough of the remaining water to form a soft, sticky dough. Increase the speed to medium and mix for a further 6 to 8 minutes until you have a soft, glossy elastic dough.

3. Add the softened butter and continue to mix for a further 4 to 5 minutes, scraping down the bowl periodically to ensure that the butter is fully incorporated. The dough will be very soft.

4. Tip the dough into a bowl, cover and chill for at least 6 hours until it is firm and you are able to shape it.

5. Line a large baking tray with parchment paper. Tip the dough on to a floured surface and divide into eight equal pieces. Roll each piece of dough into a ball and then flatten and roll into a small baton shape, approximately 8cm x 5cm. Place on the prepared baking tray, leaving room to spread. Place the tray in a clean plastic bag and leave to rise for 1 to 2 hours until doubled in size.

6. Preheat your oven to 200°C/Gas 6 and place a roasting tray in the bottom. Fill the roasting tray with hot water – this will create steam and help form a crust on the rolls. Put the rolls into the oven and bake for 20 to 25 minutes until risen and golden brown. Cool on a wire rack.

7. Cut the rolls vertically but not all the way through, like a hot dog roll. Chop the cooked bacon into bite-size pieces. Divide it among the rolls and top with grated cheese. Bake in a hot oven for 5 minutes until the cheese has melted.

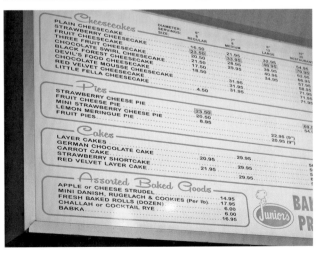

# NEW YORK-STYLE BAKED CHEESECAKE / Serves 8

Meeting Alan Rosen, third generation and co-owner of Junior's Deli in Brooklyn, has transformed the way I make a baked cheesecake. The secret to achieving the smooth, velvety texture is in the method. Always mix the filling very slowly so that you don't incorporate any air into the mixture and always bake it in a water bath. Here is my version of the classic. Like the cheesecakes made at Junior's, a sponge base is essential – don't be tempted to give it a biscuit base.

**PREP:** 30 minutes

**BAKE:** 1 hour

**CHILL:** 4 hours

### for the base:

50g self-raising flour

¼ teaspoon baking powder

a pinch of salt

2 large egg yolks

50g caster sugar

zest of ½ a lemon

30g melted unsalted butter, plus extra for greasing

2 large egg whites

¼ teaspoon cream of tartar

### for the filling:

800g full-fat cream cheese

2 tablespoons custard powder

100g caster sugar

4 medium eggs

2 teaspoons vanilla extract

235ml double cream

### equipment:

23cm spring form cake tin

1. Preheat your oven to 175°C/Gas 4. Butter a 23cm spring form cake tin.

2. To make the base, sieve the flour, baking powder and salt into a bowl and set to one side. Place the egg yolks in a large bowl and beat for 2 minutes with an electric whisk. Add 2 tablespoons of the sugar and beat until the mixture is thick and a trail of the mixture will hold its shape when dribbled on to the mix (this is called the 'ribbon stage'). It will take around 5 minutes. Add the flour mixture and fold in. Stir in the lemon zest and melted butter.

3. In a clean bowl, beat the egg whites with the cream of tartar until stiff. Gradually add the remaining sugar and beat well between additions until you have glossy white peaks. Fold the whites into the egg yolk mix carefully. Pour this into the prepared tin. Bake for 12 to 14 minutes. The base should be pale in colour and spring back when touched gently. Place the tin on a wire rack to cool, but do not remove the base from the tin. Once cool, wrap the outside of the tin in tinfoil.

4. To make the filling, take 200g of the cream cheese and place in a large bowl with the custard powder and 25g of the sugar. Beat very slowly with an electric whisk until smooth. Add another 200g of cream cheese and another 25g of sugar. Whisk again on a slow speed. You will need to keep scraping the sides of the bowl. Repeat the process two more times until all the cream cheese and sugar are incorporated. Be patient and don't be tempted to rush this stage; remember, this makes the velvety smooth texture.

5. Add the eggs, one at a time, and mix on a medium speed, beating well after each addition. Add the vanilla extract and double cream. Beat until just blended. Pour this mixture over the base. Take a roasting tray and sit the cheesecake in it. Add cold water until it comes about 2.5cm up the sides of the spring form tin. Bake for 1 hour. The edges should be slightly golden and the centre of the cheesecake should have a slight wobble. Remove the cheesecake from the baking tray and place on a wire rack to cool completely. Once cold, cover with clingfilm and place in the fridge for a minimum of 4 hours. Eat just as it is or serve with berries.

# CHOCOLATE CHEESECAKE BROWNIES / Makes 8

I loved visiting Junior's in Brooklyn and in tribute to them, I've come up with my own cheesecake recipe, which I've put together with a brownie mixture to give you the best of both worlds of these much-loved classics. A total cheesecake-brownie fest.

**PREP:** 25 minutes

**BAKE:** 35–40 minutes

**for the brownie mix:**

400g dark chocolate,
   chopped into small chunks

225g unsalted butter

3 large eggs

225g caster sugar

75g self-raising flour

½ teaspoon salt

1 teaspoon vanilla extract

**for the cheesecake mix:**

200g full-fat cream cheese

1½ teaspoons custard
   powder

15g caster sugar

1 medium egg

½ teaspoon vanilla extract

60ml double cream

**equipment:**

22cm x 29cm brownie tin

1. Line a 22cm x 29cm brownie tin with parchment paper. Preheat your oven to 180°C/Gas 4.

2. First make the brownie mix. Break 225g of the chocolate into small chunks and place in a heatproof bowl with the butter. Place over a pan of simmering water and heat until melted. Leave to cool.

3. Beat the eggs and sugar together until pale and the mixture has thickened. Add the melted chocolate and butter mixture to the eggs and stir until thoroughly combined. Fold in the flour, salt, remaining chocolate chunks and the vanilla extract. Pour into the prepared tin.

4. Next make the cheesecake mix. Using an electric whisk on a slow speed, beat the cream cheese with the custard powder, sugar, egg, vanilla extract and cream. Mix until smooth and all the ingredients are combined.

5. Drop spoonfuls of the cheesecake mix on to the brownie then, using a spatula, fold through the brownie to create swirls.

6. Bake for 35 to 40 minutes. Check after this time as ovens vary – it may need a bit longer. When it's ready, a little mixture should still stick to a skewer when inserted in the middle of the brownie.

7. Leave to cool completely before cutting into squares.

# FUN IN THE SUN /

## MIAMI

Key lime pie / Best-ever chocolate chip cookies /
Peanut butter cookies / Waffles / American pancakes /
Cuban bread / Cuban pastries

For many people, Miami conjures up thoughts of the stylish restaurants and lively nightclubs that line South Beach. I really had no idea what to expect, but the city has so much more than this on offer, particularly in the realm of food. Miami's cuisine reflects the diverse origins of its population – currently over one third of its inhabitants are of Cuban descent – and Latin America, alongside the Caribbean, heavily influences the incredible dishes to be found on these sunny streets.

When I travelled to Miami, I was lucky enough to have Nedal Ahmad guide me through Little Havana, a neighbourhood that is home to many Cuban immigrants and some really tasty dishes. Chicago-born, Miami-raised Nedal has embraced the city's Cuban and Latin influences in his award-winning restaurant, Pincho Factory. Here you can indulge in a *croquettessa*, a fried Cuban croquette patty, or a Tostón burger, which features two giant fried plantain 'buns' – this is a seriously good burger. Nedal advised me to venture to the El Brazo Fuerte Bakery, one of Miami's best pastry shops, to try some local delicacies. Here I had *pastelitos*, baked puff-pastry pasties infused with anything from guava to ham, and it's easy to see why they're so popular – try my recipe on page 236. Inspired by all the delicious bakes El Brazo Fuerte has to offer, I also decided to create my very own Cuban bread recipe – have a look on page 232.

Whilst in Miami, I was not only lucky enough to visit the Biltmore Hotel, the centrepiece of the elegant, palatial resort of Coral Gables, but to get back into my whites and work with their pastry team on the quintessential Miami pudding – Key lime pie. Built in the 1920s, the Biltmore was once one of the most fashionable resorts in the entire country, and it made the perfect setting to enjoy this decadent dessert. Tangy, sweet, sharp and creamy – no wonder it's a Florida favourite. You can find my take on this classic on page 223. Joe's Stone Crab on Miami Beach serves a fantastic slice and their food is some of the best I've had in years. From coconut shrimp in hollerback sauce to wild oysters and huge, meaty crab claws, their menu is bursting with some incredible fresh fish and exciting flavours. No wonder this is one of the city's most famous restaurants, loved by locals and sought out by tourists.

In this chapter, I've included just a few of my baking highlights from Miami – try them yourself for a taste of this incredibly vibrant and beautiful cosmopolitan city.

# KEY LIME PIE / Serves 6

No other dessert says Florida more than Key lime pie. A biscuit base is combined with a smooth creamy topping flavoured with the sharpness of Key limes. I just love the tangy flavour. I worked my way through a few slices whilst in Miami; some were too sweet, others too sharp. This recipe gives the perfect balance, and you don't need the small Key limes from the Florida Keys to make it – regular limes work just as well.

**PREP:** 20 minutes

**BAKE:** 25–30 minutes

**CHILL:** 2 hours

**for the base:**

200g plain Hobnob or
   digestive biscuits

100g melted unsalted butter

**for the filling:**

4 egg yolks

1 x 397g tin of
   condensed milk

zest and juice of 4 limes

**to serve:**

400ml cream, whipped

extra lime zest

**equipment:**

20cm loose bottom
   sandwich tin

1.  Place the biscuits in a food processor and pulse until they are crushed but not too fine. Tip into a bowl, add the melted butter and stir to combine. Press into the base of a 20cm loose bottom sandwich tin. Push up the sides of the tin to create a crust about 3cm high. Place in the fridge to set.

2.  Preheat your oven to 150°C/Gas 2.

3.  To make the filling, whisk the egg yolks with the condensed milk. Add the lime juice and zest and whisk again. Pour into the prepared base. Bake for 25 to 30 minutes or until just set. The filling will have risen and may have started to colour around the edges.

4.  Remove from the oven and leave to cool at room temperature. Chill in the fridge for at least 2 hours before serving. Serve a wedge of cooled pie with the whipped cream and a little more lime zest sprinkled over the top.

# BEST-EVER CHOCOLATE CHIP COOKIES / Makes 16 cookies

The first ever chocolate chip cookie was invented in America in 1930 at the Toll House Inn restaurant in Massachusetts. Now a firm favourite across the world, the chocolate chip cookie is the most popular type of home-baked cookie in the States. Big, soft and chewy, they are a treat for kids – especially big kids like me! This recipe will give you delicious cookies that are much better than any shop-bought version. The secret to the flavour is to use the best dark chocolate chips you can find.

**PREP:** 15 minutes

**CHILL:** 2 hours

**BAKE:** 12–15 minutes

150g softened unsalted butter

150g caster sugar

100g light soft brown sugar

1 large egg

250g plain flour

1 teaspoon baking powder

½ teaspoon salt

45g cocoa powder

150g dark chocolate chips

1. In a large bowl, cream the butter and both sugars together with an electric whisk until smooth and fluffy. Add the egg and mix well.

2. In a separate bowl, mix the flour with the baking powder, salt and cocoa powder. Add to the butter mixture and mix well to form a stiff dough. At first it will look like there is too much flour, but whisk slowly and it will form a stiff dough. Add the chocolate chips.

3. Tip the dough on to a large piece of clingfilm or greaseproof paper. Roll the dough into a cylinder shape 27cm long and 6cm wide. Place in the fridge to firm up for at least 2 hours.

4. Line two baking trays with parchment paper. Preheat your oven to 160°C/Gas 3.

5. Unwrap the dough, cut into 16 equal slices and place on the prepared trays, leaving room to spread. Bake for 12 to 15 minutes. The cookies should have risen and spread out. They will still be soft when you remove them from the oven, so leave to firm on the tray for a few minutes before cooling completely on a wire rack.

# PEANUT BUTTER COOKIES /

Makes 16 cookies

Following a very close second to their cousin the chocolate chip cookie, these cookies are also very American, devilishly moreish and straightforward to make. For a coarser texture you can use crunchy peanut butter.

**PREP:** 15 minutes

**CHILL:** 2 hours

**BAKE:** 14–16 minutes

160g softened unsalted butter

275g smooth peanut butter

135g caster sugar

135g light soft brown sugar

2 medium eggs

275g plain flour

1 teaspoon baking powder

½ teaspoon salt

1.  In a large bowl cream the butter, peanut butter and sugars together with an electric whisk until smooth and fluffy. Add the eggs one at a time and mix well after each addition.

2.  In a separate bowl, mix the flour with the baking powder and salt. Add to the butter mixure and mix well to form a stiff dough.

3.  Tip the dough on to a large sheet of greaseproof paper or clingfilm and roll it into a cylinder shape 28cm long and 9cm wide. Place in the fridge for at least 2 hours to firm up.

4.  Line two baking trays with parchment paper. Preheat your oven to 160°C/Gas 3.

5.  Unwrap the dough, cut it into 16 equal slices and place on the prepared trays. Bake for 14 to 16 minutes. The cookies should be golden, risen and slightly cracked on the surface. They will be soft when you remove them from the oven, so leave to firm up on the tray for a few minutes before cooling completely on a wire rack.

# WAFFLES / Makes 6

In Europe waffles are a sweet treat – the honeycomb pattern being a great carrier for syrup, whipped cream and oozing chocolate sauce – whilst in America I had them for breakfast. Four waffles served with scrambled eggs, bacon, ketchup and maple syrup certainly sets you up for the day. My recipe below is for plain waffles and they can be topped with whatever takes your fancy, whether you choose to serve them European- or American-style. You will need to have a waffle iron or maker for this recipe.

**PREP:** 10 minutes

**COOK:** 4–6 minutes
  per batch

300g plain flour

1½ teaspoons baking powder

½ teaspoon salt

50g caster sugar

2 medium eggs

415ml full-fat milk

90g melted unsalted butter

oil spray

**equipment:**

waffle iron or maker

1. In a large bowl, mix together the flour, baking powder, salt and sugar.

2. In a separate bowl or jug, beat the eggs with the milk. Gradually pour the mixture on to the dry ingredients and beat until you have a smooth batter. Finally, stir in the melted butter.

3. Heat your waffle iron or maker and spray it with oil. Once the iron is hot, pour a ladleful of batter on to the waffle iron and cook until golden. Repeat with the remaining batter. Serve warm.

# AMERICAN PANCAKES /

Makes 6–8

Like Scotch pancakes or drop scones, American pancakes are thick and spongy. They are delicious spread with butter or drizzled with golden syrup. It's also worth trying them for breakfast American-style with streaky bacon and maple syrup.

**PREP:** 10 minutes

**COOK:** 3–4 minutes
per pancake

125g plain flour

1½ tablespoons caster sugar

1 teaspoon baking powder

½ teaspoon bicarbonate
of soda

½ teaspoon salt

1 medium egg

175ml buttermilk

2 tablespoons melted
unsalted butter,
slightly cooled

1–2 tablespoons vegetable
oil, to fry

1. Place the flour, sugar, baking powder, bicarbonate of soda and salt in a mixing bowl. Stir to combine.

2. In a jug, beat the egg, buttermilk and melted butter together. Pour this on to the dry ingredients and stir until you have a smooth, thick batter.

3. Heat a heavy-based frying pan over a medium heat. Brush the surface with a little vegetable oil. Add two tablespoonfuls of the batter per pancake to the pan. Once bubbles begin appearing on the surface of the pancake, turn it over and cook the other side. Repeat using all the batter. The pancakes should be fluffy and golden brown. Serve straight away or keep them warm on a low heat in the oven.

# CUBAN BREAD / Makes 2 loaves

As Miami has a large Cuban population, this bread is a staple that is available everywhere. I must admit, in appearance it does look slightly boring as it resembles an unslashed baguette without the crunchy crust. But I was blown away by the flavour! It also has a longer shelf life than that of a baguette due to the fat content. It's a great loaf for sandwich-making and is used a lot in Miami for panini-style sandwiches, which are pressed between hot irons.

**PREP:** 20 minutes

**PROVE:** 2–4 hours

**BAKE:** 30 minutes

350g strong white bread flour, plus extra for dusting

7g salt

7g instant yeast

30g lard

175–200ml water

oil, for greasing

**equipment:**

a baguette tray or a large baking tray

1. Place the flour in a large mixing bowl. Add the salt to one side and the yeast to the other. Add the lard and three quarters of the water and turn the mixture around with your fingers. Continue to add the remaining water, a little at a time, until all the flour and lard are incorporated and you have a rough dough. You may not need all the water.

2. Tip the dough on to a lightly floured surface and knead for 5 to 10 minutes until you have a soft, smooth dough. Place in a lightly greased bowl, cover and leave to prove for 1 to 3 hours or until doubled in size.

3. Line a large baking tray with parchment paper or use a baguette tray. Take the dough and tip on to a lightly floured surface. Divide into two equal pieces. Shape one piece of dough into a rectangle by flattening the dough and folding the sides into the middle. Roll up into a sausage shape – the top should be smooth and the seam should run along the base. Starting with your hands in the middle, roll the sausage to the length of the tray. Repeat with the other piece of dough. Place on the tray, then place the tray in a clean plastic bag and leave to prove for about an hour or until doubled in size.

4. Preheat your oven to 200°C/Gas 6. When the bread is ready, bake for 30 minutes or until golden brown and cooked through. Cool on a wire rack.

# CUBAN PASTRIES / Makes 8

*Pastelitos* are baked puff pastries that are filled with sweet or savoury flavours; cleverly, they are made in different shapes to identify what's inside. Seek them out at El Brazo Fuerte in the Little Havana district of Miami. Opened 35 years ago, it's one of Miami's best Cuban/French bakeries. Traditional *pastelito* fillings include cream cheese with guava and coconut – sounds a bit strange, but it's delicious. Savoury fillings are mainly beef, but also chicken, ham and cheese. In the cafés of Miami, these little pastries are eaten any time of the day, served with very strong Cuban coffee.

This recipe is my take on the traditional *pastelitos de guayaba*. The guava has the appearance of bright pink jam with a flavour of tropical fruit juice. Here I have used rhubarb, for its sharpness and texture, mixed with a guava juice reduction. Tongue-tingling and delicious – the flavours will instantly take you to the beaches of Miami.

**PREP:** 1 hour

**CHILL:** 11 hours

**BAKE:** 20–25 minutes

**for the puff pastry:**

100g strong white bread flour, plus extra for dusting

100g plain flour

a pinch of fine salt

75–100ml very cold water

165g cold unsalted butter

**for the filling:**

200g rhubarb, cut into 1.5cm chunks

75g caster sugar

75ml guava, or similar tropical fruit, juice

2 tablespoons arrowroot

1 beaten egg, to glaze

1. Combine the flours and salt in a bowl. Mix in enough water to form a reasonably tight but still kneadable dough. Turn out on to a lightly floured surface and knead for 5 to 10 minutes until smooth. Form the dough into a rough rectangle, wrap in clingfilm and place in the fridge for at least 7 hours.

2. Using a rolling pin, bash the butter on a floured surface to flatten it to a rectangle 20cm long and just less than 12cm wide. Wrap in clingfilm and chill in the fridge.

3. Roll out the chilled dough to a 12cm x 30cm rectangle. Lay the chilled butter on the dough so it covers the bottom two thirds. Make sure it's positioned neatly and comes almost to the edges of the dough.

4. Lift the exposed dough at the top and fold down over half of the butter. Fold the butter-covered bottom half of dough over the top. You will now have a sandwich of two layers of butter and three of dough. Seal the edges by pressing or pinching them together. Wrap in clingfilm and chill in the fridge for an hour.

5. Remove the dough and turn it 90 degrees so you have a short end towards you, then roll it into a long rectangle. Fold the top quarter down and the bottom quarter up so they meet in the middle. Then fold the dough in half along the centre line and press or pinch the edges together to seal. Wrap in clingfilm and chill for an hour.

6. Remove the dough, turn it 90 degrees so a short end is facing you, then roll it into a long rectangle. Fold one third down, then fold the bottom third up over the top. Press or pinch the edges to seal. Wrap the pastry and chill for an hour.

7. Repeat the last stage of rolling, folding and chilling. The dough is now ready to use.

8. To make the filling, place the rhubarb in a pan with the sugar and fruit juice and gently bring to a simmer. Cook until the rhubarb is soft but still holds its shape. Remove the rhubarb with a slotted spoon and set aside. Mix the arrowroot with a splash of water to loosen. Pour into the warm fruit juice. Stir and bring to the boil, then cook until the sauce thickens. Return the rhubarb to the pan and stir to coat in the thick syrup. Tip into a clean bowl, cover with clingfilm and leave to go cold and set like a jam.

9. Preheat your oven to 200°C/Gas 6 and line two baking trays with parchment paper.

10. On a lightly floured surface, roll the dough into a rectangle approximately 40cm x 20cm. Trim to neaten. Cut into eight equal squares. Place a spoonful of rhubarb filling in the middle of each square. Brush the edges with water. Take one corner and fold it over to meet the opposite corner and make a triangle. Press the edges together to seal. Make a small slit in the top of each pastry to let the steam escape. Place on the prepared trays. Brush with egg wash and bake for 20 to 25 minutes until golden brown and risen. Leave to cool before eating.

# PRIDE OF POLAND /

## WARSAW

Nalesniki Ruskie / Babka / Forest moss cake /
Polish cheesecake / Beetroot cake / Polish chalka bread

Warsaw has an incredibly rich history and really interesting culinary practices. After it was destroyed in World War II, the old town was rebuilt exactly as it used to be. It therefore has a lovely vibe to it – really pretty streets and some great places to stop and eat. This is where I visited the iconic Pod Barbakanem milk bar, where elderly Polish ladies are busy at the serving hatch. Milk bars have been an important part of Polish culture for the last 50 years. It was here that I tried classic Polish potato pancakes (see page 243).

Stopping off to warm up in a café in the old town, I was served the most delicious green cake. It took me a while to figure out its ingredients as it wasn't overly sweet but it was so moreish. The green colour came from spinach; a 'healthy' cake of sorts with a fairytale name – 'forest moss cake'. Layered with sour cream, it is studded with pomegranate seeds, which give a refreshing pop to each mouthful. My version is on page 247 and I've added a layer of pistachios to it which work incredibly well.

There is also a modern, post-war part of Warsaw, which is where I visited Odette, the hot new patisserie run by Jarek Nowakowski. It felt like the place had been styled right out of an episode of *Mad Men*. Jarek's pastry skills are second to none – he is really bringing things to another level by introducing modern twists when using traditional Polish ingredients.

A quirky place to visit for a slice of potato cheesecake is Café Misianka, which is in a converted toilet block in the Skaryszewski park. It is run by a lovely lady who has been there for years and has made a very good business for herself. Traditionally, cheap potatoes were used to pad out the more expensive dairy ingredients.

The Piwonski Bakery opened in 1955 and is now run by the third generation of the same family. Grandfather Piwonski hid in the bakery to escape the Nazis, keep warm and find food. He ended up working there, then owning it, and his son now runs it with his two daughters. The ovens they use are huge floor-to-ceiling ones which are on for 24 hours a day. It takes a team of three to run them, as there can be up to 300 loaves in them at any one time. Their signature loaf is the plaited *chalka* bread, for which I've given you a recipe on page 254.

The baking scene in Poland is very exciting and I was so glad I got the chance to go and experience it for myself. With their country's signature bakes, the Poles certainly do have something to be extremely proud of.

# NALESNIKI RUSKIE / Makes 6–8

I sampled these 'Russian pancakes' in a popular milk bar in Warsaw. Milk bars are cafés where the menu is based on dairy products, but they also serve traditional Polish dishes such as soups and dumplings. When Poland became communist, the people were poor. The milk bars thrived as they offered cheap, hearty meals for workers. All meals containing dairy, vegetables and grains are still subsidised by the government and the food is very cheap. Whilst I was there people from all walks of life came in for lunch: families, workers and homeless people all ate together in the simple café.

**PREP:** 30 minutes

**COOK:** 5 minutes per pancake

**for the filling:**

275g potatoes, unpeeled

1 small onion, peeled and finely chopped

½ tablespoon sunflower oil or a knob of butter

150g curd cheese or cottage cheese

salt and ground white pepper

**for the basic pancake batter:**

125g plain flour

½ teaspoon salt

2 medium eggs

150ml full-fat milk

1½ tablespoons sunflower oil, plus extra for greasing

**equipment:**

20cm frying pan

1. To make the filling, boil the potatoes in their skins in salted water. Cook until soft enough to mash (the time this takes will depend on the size of your potatoes). Remove from the pan and leave to cool.

2. Gently fry the chopped onion in a little oil or butter until soft, but not coloured.

3. Once the potatoes are cooked, peel and pass through a ricer. Add the cooked onion and curd cheese and season well with salt and white pepper. Mix together, then leave to one side.

4. To make the pancakes, place the flour and salt in a mixing bowl. Make a well in the middle and crack the eggs into it. Using a wooden spoon begin to mix, incorporating the flour from the edge of the bowl. As the mixture thickens, gradually add the milk. Mix well after each addition of milk and continue until all the milk is incorporated and you have a smooth batter. Stir in the oil.

5. Heat a frying pan at least 20cm in diameter over a medium to high heat. Pour a little oil on to a wad of kitchen paper and lightly wipe the base of the pan to grease it.

6. Pour a little batter (around 3 tablespoons) into the middle of the pan, tip the pan from side to side and swirl the batter around until the base of the pan is covered. Cook for approximately 30 to 45 seconds, then loosen the edge with a palette knife, flip the pancake over and cook the other side for another 30 to 45 seconds. The pancake should be golden brown.

7. Slide out of the pan on to greaseproof paper and repeat until all the batter is finished. Stack the pancakes between greaseproof paper until ready to use.

8. To assemble, take a pancake and place a large spoon of potato curd filling in the middle, fold in half, then in half again to make a triangle. Place this back in a warm pan and cook for around 2 minutes on each side. Eat straight away.

# BABKA / Serves 10–12

*Babka* means 'cake' and it comes in many types in Poland. Whilst there, I met up with chef Jarek Nowakowski, who has worked in many Michelin-starred restaurants in Europe. He has now returned to Warsaw where he has set up a very contemporary patisserie called Odette, producing exceptional desserts using premium ingredients. A very passionate baker, he is proud of his new venture and of showcasing his work. He was happy to share his recipe for *babka* with me, which is a non-yeasted sponge cake. New to me is the addition of glucose in the mixture. This helps to keep the cake moist. Jarek makes individual ones but my recipe is for a large one which can easily be cut into portions.

**PREP:** 20 minutes

**BAKE:** 50 minutes–1 hour

90g softened unsalted butter, plus extra for greasing

215g plain flour, plus extra for dusting

150g desiccated coconut

250g caster sugar

5 medium eggs

55g liquid glucose or runny honey

1½ teaspoons baking powder

150ml double cream

zest of 1 lemon

zest of 2 limes

3 tablespoons jam (your favourite flavour)

**for the icing:**

200g icing sugar, sieved

2–4 tablespoons lemon juice

lemon zest and dried rose petals, to garnish

**equipment:**

22cm square tin

1. Grease a 22cm square tin with butter, dust with flour, then line with parchment paper. Preheat your oven to 160°C/Gas 3.

2. Spread the coconut out in a thin layer on a baking tray and bake for 5 to 10 minutes. Remove and leave to cool.

3. Place the butter and caster sugar in a large bowl and cream together until the sugar has dissolved and the mixture is pale. Add the eggs one at a time, blending well after each addition. Add the glucose and mix well. Sieve the flour and baking powder together and fold into the mixture to incorporate. Add the toasted coconut and the cream and mix well. Finally, stir in the lemon and lime zest.

4. Pour half the mixture into the prepared tin and smooth to level. Put spoonfuls of jam, evenly spaced, on to the mixture, then cover with the remaining cake mix. Smooth the top to level and bake for 50 to 60 minutes until the cake is golden and well risen. Leave to cool on a wire rack.

5. To make the icing, mix the icing sugar and lemon juice together to form a smooth paste.

6. Remove the cake from the tin. Brush the top with the icing and scatter over the lemon zest and dried rose petals.

# FOREST MOSS CAKE /

Makes 1 large cake

This is a really pretty cake – bright green and decorated with jewels of pomegranate – that I discovered in a café. The cake has a very light texture and the green colour comes from spinach, so it's healthy too! It sounds odd, but it's really lovely with the soured cream filling.

**PREP:** 20 minutes

**BAKE:** 40–45 minutes

**CHILL:** 1 hour

200g frozen spinach

butter, for greasing

225g plain flour

2 teaspoons baking powder

3 medium eggs

340g caster sugar

200ml sunflower oil

1 teaspoon vanilla extract

**for the filling:**

300g mascarpone cheese

150ml soured cream

25g icing sugar

**for the topping:**

30g pistachios

2 tablespoons pomegranate seeds

**equipment:**

23cm loose bottom tart tin

1. Place the frozen spinach in a sieve over a bowl. Leave to defrost, then squeeze it against the sieve a few times to get rid of the moisture, pat dry and chop finely.

2. Grease and line the base of a 23cm loose bottom cake tin with parchment paper. Preheat your oven to 180°C/Gas 4.

3. Sieve the flour and baking powder together.

4. In a large bowl, whisk the eggs and caster sugar together until pale, thick and fluffy. Gradually add the oil and vanilla extract and whisk to combine. Add the spinach and stir to combine. Fold in the flour until thoroughly combined.

5. Pour the mixture into the prepared tin and bake for 40 to 45 minutes until the cake is risen and golden and has come away from the sides of the tin. Leave to cool in the tin for 5 minutes, then remove from the tin and leave to cool on a wire rack.

6. To make the filling, beat the mascarpone until soft and smooth. Add the soured cream and icing sugar and stir until you have a smooth cream filling. Chill in the fridge until ready to use.

7. To assemble the cake, remove the top third so the cake is level. Place the base on a serving plate. Spread the mascarpone filling over the base.

8. In a food processor, blitz the pistachios until finely chopped. Add the top third of the cake to the processor and blitz until you make nutty crumbs. Sprinkle the nutty crumbs over the creamy filling. You should have a thick amount of crumb. Decorate with the pomegranate seeds.

9. Put the cake into the fridge for an hour before serving so the crumb settles and the filling firms up.

# POLISH CHEESECAKE / Serves 9

Slabs of cheesecake can be seen in all Polish bakeries, but the best one I tasted was in Café Misianka, a tiny café in a park in Warsaw. The building is in fact an old 1920s toilet block and is run by Misha, a self-taught baker. Having started with the café, she now has many outlets all over the city selling her beautiful and delicious cakes – a very enterprising lady! Her cheesecake is made in the traditional Polish way: no base or crust, just cheese, eggs, butter, sugar and, wait for it, mashed potato! It really is light, silky smooth and delicious.

**PREP:** 30 minutes

**BAKE:** 30–35 minutes

2 medium-sized potatoes

3 large eggs, separated

100g caster sugar

600g full-fat cream cheese

40g softened unsalted butter

1 tablespoon custard powder

zest of 1 lemon

zest of 1 orange

icing sugar, for dusting

**equipment:**

20cm square cake tin

1. Line a 20cm square cake tin with baking parchment. Preheat your oven to 170°C/Gas 3.

2. Boil the potatoes in their skins in salted water. Cook until soft enough to mash (the time this takes will depend on the size of your potatoes). Remove from the pan and leave to cool. Peel and pass through a ricer. This helps get the silky smooth texture of the cheesecake.

3. In a large bowl, whisk the egg yolks with the caster sugar until the mixture thickens and turns pale.

4. In a separate bowl, whisk the egg whites to soft peaks.

5. Place the mashed potatoes, cream cheese, butter, custard powder and zests in a food processor. Pulse until the ingredients are just blended together. Do not over mix.

6. Add a third of the cream cheese mixture to the egg yolk mixture and whisk to combine. Continue adding the cream cheese a third at a time and whisk until it's all combined and there are no lumps. Stop mixing as soon as it is incorporated. Fold in the egg whites until you have a smooth, airy mixture.

7. Pour into the prepared tin and bake for 30 to 35 minutes. The cheesecake should be just set and pale golden brown in colour. Turn the oven off, leave the oven door slightly open and leave to cool completely.

8. Remove from the tin and cut into portions. Dust with icing sugar and eat on its own or with berries.

# BEETROOT CAKE / Serves 8–10

Beetroot is a staple ingredient in Polish cooking; it is so versatile that it can be used to make delicious moist cakes. This recipe is full of flavour and the frosting gives it a light, creamy contrast that is just right. If you have some rose petals to hand, they always look nice as a finishing touch.

**PREP:** 20 minutes

**BAKE:** 45 minutes–1 hour

100ml sunflower oil, plus
  extra for greasing

200g cooked beetroot
  (not in vinegar),
  roughly chopped

200g dark soft brown sugar

200g self-raising flour

½ teaspoon baking powder

½ teaspoon bicarbonate
  of soda

25g cocoa powder, plus
  extra for dusting

1 teaspoon vanilla extract

200ml soured cream

125g dark chocolate chips

cocoa powder, for dusting

**for the frosting:**

150g cream cheese

50g softened unsalted butter

75g icing sugar

**equipment:**

2lb (900g) loaf tin

1. Grease and line a 2lb (900g) loaf tin. Preheat your oven to 180°C/Gas 4.

2. Use a food processor to purée the beetroot with the oil and brown sugar. Tip this into a mixing bowl.

3. Sieve the self-raising flour with the baking powder, bicarbonate of soda and cocoa. Fold the flour mix into the beetroot purée and stir to combine. Add the vanilla extract, soured cream and chocolate chips and mix thoroughly. Pour into the prepared tin, smooth the top with a palette knife, and bake for 45 minutes to an hour.

4. Test to see if the cake is cooked by inserting a skewer into the centre – it should come out clean. Leave to cool in the tin for 10 minutes, then remove from the tin and leave to cool completely on a wire rack.

5. To make the frosting, beat the cream cheese and butter together. Add the icing sugar a little at a time and mix until you have a smooth frosting. Spread the frosting on top of the cake and dust lightly with cocoa powder.

# POLISH CHALKA BREAD /

**Makes 4 small loaves**

I was lucky enough to work the ceramic ovens at the Piwonski bakery in Warsaw. The ovens were rescued from a fire in the bakery in 1959 and Grandfather Piwonski reopened it in 1962. Today Paul Piwonski and his daughters carry on the tradition by making bread the same way their grandfather did, with natural ingredients and traditional methods. Paul believes his bread tastes great because it is baked in these ovens. They can hold up to 300 loaves and it takes a three-man crew to unload the loaves once baked. It's very hot, hard work. In the prep room at the back of the bakery, a line of men roll and plait the *chalka* loaves. Here is my recipe for you to try.

**PREP:** 20 minutes

**PROVE:** 2–4 hours

**BAKE:** 15 minutes

500g strong white bread flour, plus extra for dusting

7g salt

20g caster sugar

7g instant yeast

25g softened unsalted butter

2 medium eggs, beaten

120ml warm full-fat milk

110ml water

oil, for greasing

1 beaten egg, to glaze

1. Place the flour in a large bowl. Add the salt and sugar to one side and the yeast to the other. Add the butter, 2 beaten eggs and milk. Turn the mixture around with your fingers to pick up the ingredients from the side of the bowl. Slowly add enough water to form a soft dough.

2. Tip the dough on to a lightly floured surface and knead for 5 to 10 minutes. Work through the wet stage until you have soft, smooth ball of dough. Place in a lightly oiled bowl, cover and leave to prove for 1 to 3 hours or until doubled in size.

3. Line two baking trays with parchment paper.

4. Tip the dough on to a lightly floured surface. Fold the dough in on itself to knock it back and remove the air. Divide into four equal pieces.

5. Divide each piece of dough into five equal pieces weighing approximately 40g each. Roll each of these into ropes measuring 30cm. Try to keep each rope the same length and thickness. The trick is not to roll them in too much flour – this makes it more difficult. Lay five ropes vertically in front of you. Pinch the ends together at the top to join them. Now you are ready to plait. Starting from the left, the ropes are numbered 1 to 5:

6. Take the outside rope on the right (5) and place it over the rope next to it (4). Then take the middle rope (3) and place it over rope 4. Now do the same starting from the left. Take rope 1 and place it over the rope next to it (2). Take the middle rope (3) and place it over rope 2. Now repeat the sequence until you get to the bottom: 5 over 4; 3 over 4; 1 over 2; 3 over 2.

7. Once you get to the bottom, pinch the ends together and tuck them underneath. Now make three other small loaves in the same way.

8. Place the loaves on the prepared trays, cover and leave to rise for about an hour. Preheat your oven to 200°C/Gas 6.

9. Just before baking, brush the loaves with beaten egg. Bake for 15 minutes until risen and golden brown. Cool on a wire rack.

# THE RUSSIAN OVEN /

## ST PETERSBURG

Russian pies / Blinis / Medovik /
Vatrushka / Sweet berry pancakes

This was my first ever trip to Russia and I was blown away by the beauty of St Petersburg. I think it's the prettiest place I've ever been to, the snow making it seem like a magical fairytale. Even though the statues get covered in boxes for protection during the winter, it's still breathtaking. I'll never forget being driven around the grounds of St Catherine's Palace in a horse and carriage. The temperature was -27°C – the coldest I've ever been – but it was so exhilarating. Thank goodness I had my thermals and furry winter hat with me.

I hadn't formed any ideas about the Russian baking scene, so it was really exciting to land there and explore. When I went into the café at the palace, I noticed they were selling what looked like little flat doughnuts with a cheese filling, but I could see they were made from dough. I just had to try one; it turns out that they are the most moreish cheesy-filled snacks called *vatrushkas* and are eaten across Russia. I've given you a recipe for them on page 269.

What I didn't expect to find was that the Russians produce exceptional and unique pies. I visited a bakery called Stolle, which is like a posh Greggs, and they have branches all over Russia as well as internationally. There is a UK branch in London if you fancy trying one of their intricately decorated pies, or you can have a go at making your own using my recipes on pages 260–63. The unusual thing about the pastry used for these pies is that it is like a Danish pastry, so you get the sweetness of the pastry alongside savoury fillings. I've given you two recipes – one meat and one vegetarian – which both work so well. They are almost too beautiful to eat!

If you get a chance to visit St Petersburg then do try and get to see some of the grand architecture, like the palace, and definitely St Isaac's Square, which has the bronze statue of Peter the Great in the middle of it. The Hotel Astoria is on one side of the square and I was lucky enough to visit their kitchens. Then I was given a huge blanket to wrap myself up in whilst I stood outside on a famous balcony from which Lenin gave a speech in 1919.

*Medovik*, or honey cake, is a favourite traditional Russian cake. Seen in all bakeries, it's not like anything I've tried before. It goes biscuity once baked, so the key is to let it soften in the fridge once it has been layered up with its creamy filling, but it's definitely worth the wait. There's a lovely story about how it was invented as well, so have a look at page 267.

I definitely want to revisit St Petersburg, and other places in this vast country as well. I feel that I only just managed to scratch the surface with what I found on my short break over there.

# RUSSIAN PIES / Serves 4–6

I had never seen anything like the array of pies on display at the Russian bakery Stolle. Baked to classic recipes, each one is highly decorated. The pastry is made from an enriched yeasted dough, which includes a small amount of vodka, and it's laminated with layers of butter. Stolle sell fruit, fish, meat, cabbage and other vegetarian pies, each with its own shape and distinctive elaborate decoration. The recipes are secret, but I have created my own versions for you to try – a meat one below and a vegetarian option on the next page.

## BEEF PIE

**PREP:** 30 minutes

**PROVE:** 6½ hours

**CHILL:** 12 hours

**COOK:** 1½ hours

**BAKE:** 45 minutes

**for the dough:**

375g strong white bread flour, plus extra for dusting

7g salt

80g caster sugar

7g yeast

1 large egg

70ml water

1 tablespoon vodka

75ml full-fat milk

30g melted unsalted butter, plus extra for greasing

180g unsalted butter

1. Put the flour into the bowl of a mixer fitted with a dough hook. Add the salt and sugar to one side of the bowl and the yeast to the other.

2. Add the egg, water, vodka and milk and mix on a slow speed for 2 minutes until all the ingredients combine and you have a dough. Increase the speed to medium and mix for 5 minutes until you have a soft, glossy elastic dough. Add the melted butter and mix for another 2 minutes until it's incorporated into the dough.

3. Tip the dough into a bowl greased with butter, cover and leave to prove until doubled in size. This can take up to 6 hours.

4. Flatten the 180g of butter into a rectangle approximately 27cm x 14cm. Place in the fridge. Tip out the dough and, on a lightly floured surface, roll it into a rectangle approximately 40cm x 15cm.

5. Place the butter on the dough so it covers the bottom two thirds of the dough. Ensure that the butter is positioned neatly and comes almost to the edges.

6. Fold the exposed dough down over one third of the butter. Now cut off the exposed bit of butter without cutting through the dough. Place it on top of the dough you have just folded down. Fold the bottom half of the dough up. Pinch the edges to seal in the butter. Wrap in clingfilm and place in the fridge for an hour to harden.

7. Unwrap the dough and place on a lightly floured surface with the short end towards you. Roll into a rectangle approximately 40cm x 15cm. Fold up half the dough and fold down the other half so they meet in the middle, then fold over so the top half is on top of the other half. This is a book turn. Wrap and chill for an hour.

### for the filling:

550g stewing beef, cut into 2cm chunks

1 large onion, peeled and finely diced

350–400ml beef stock

2 large hard-boiled eggs, shelled and finely chopped

salt and black pepper

2 egg yolks, to glaze

8. Put the dough on to a lightly floured surface with the short end facing towards you. Roll the dough out again and repeat the book turn. Chill for another hour. Repeat twice more so you have four book turns in total. Place in the fridge and leave to chill for 8 hours.

9. To make the beef filling, place the beef and diced onion in a saucepan. Add enough stock to just cover the meat, and bring to a simmer. Cover with a lid and simmer very gently for 1½ hours. After this time the meat should be very tender. Drain the meat and onions – you can save the stock to make gravy. Leave to cool. Place the cooled filling in the bowl of a food processor. Season with a little salt and black pepper and pulse a couple of times until the filling has the texture of a coarse pâté. Tip into a mixing bowl and add the finely chopped boiled eggs. Stir so the eggs are evenly distributed. Taste and adjust the seasoning to your liking by adding more salt and pepper if required. Form into a cylinder shape approximately 22cm x 5cm and wrap tightly in clingfilm. Leave to chill in the fridge.

10. To assemble the beef pie, roll out the dough into a rectangle 5mm thick. Cut out a 26cm x 17cm rectangle. Save the trimmings to make the decorations. Brush the long edges with egg wash. Unwrap the meat cylinder and sit in the middle of the dough base. Bring the long edges up around the filling so they meet at the top. Starting on top in the centre, pinch the dough together to seal. When you reach the ends, tuck them into the sides of the parcel. Turn the parcel over so the join is now underneath. Place on a heavy-duty baking sheet or baking tray lined with parchment paper. Brush with the egg wash.

11. To make the decorations, roll the trimmings to 3mm thick. Cut out flowers and long strips of dough. Feather the edges of the strips by cutting into the dough at angles but not all the way through, creating a fringe effect. Lay the decorations across the surface of the pie. Brush with more egg wash and leave to prove for 30 minutes.

12. Preheat your oven to 200°C/Gas 6.

13. Bake your pie for 20 minutes, then lower the oven temperature to 180°C/Gas 4 and cook for a further 20 to 25 minutes. If the pastry darkens too quickly, cover loosely with foil towards the end of baking. The pastry should be deep golden brown, crisp and cooked through.

14. Leave the pie to stand for 5 to 10 minutes before slicing. It can be eaten warm or cold.

# MUSHROOM, SPINACH AND POTATO PIE

**PREP:** 30 minutes

**PROVE:** 6½ hours

**CHILL:** 12 hours

**COOK:** 20 minutes

**BAKE:** 45 minutes

**for the dough:**

1x dough recipe
  (see page 260)

**for the filling:**

400g potatoes

30g unsalted butter

1 tablespoon sunflower oil

salt and black pepper

300g chestnut mushrooms,
  sliced

100g cream cheese

50g mature Cheddar cheese,
  grated

a little fresh nutmeg

30g baby spinach leaves

2 egg yolks, to glaze

1. For the dough, see steps 1–7 on page 260.

2. To make the mushroom, spinach and potato filling, peel the potatoes and cook in boiling salted water until just cooked but not soft or falling apart. Drain and when cooled, slice into discs 5mm thick. Heat a large frying pan and melt the butter with the oil. Season the mushrooms and cook until just tender but not browned. Drain on kitchen paper and leave to cool. Beat the cream cheese with the Cheddar cheese. Season with salt, pepper and freshly grated nutmeg.

3. To assemble the mushroom, potato and spinach pie, roll the dough into a large rectangle approximately 5mm thick. Cut out a 23cm square base and place on a heavy-duty baking sheet or baking tray lined with parchment paper. Save the offcuts of the dough. Lay the potato slices across the base, going right to the edges. Next, place a layer of the cooked mushrooms over the potatoes. Spread the cream cheese mix over the mushrooms. Top with the spinach.

4. Roll the trimmings and cut out four 23cm x 5cm rectangles. Slash the edges to make a fringe. Place these to one side. Roll out the remaining pastry and cut into 3cm x 20cm strips. Slash one side to create a fringing effect. Lay these strips diagonally across the top of the pie, half in one direction and the others the other way, creating a crisscross pattern over the filling. Brush with egg wash. Take the four reserved rectangles and place each of these on the sides of the filling, creating a border – use a little egg wash as an adhesive. Pinch the dough at the corners to seal. Brush with egg wash and leave to prove for 30 minutes.

5. Preheat your oven to 200°C/Gas 6.

6. Bake your pie for 20 minutes, then lower the oven temperature to 180°C/Gas 4 and cook for a further 20 to 25 minutes. If the pastry darkens too quickly, cover loosely with foil towards the end of baking. The pastry should be deep golden brown, crisp and cooked through.

7. Leave the pie to stand for 5 to 10 minutes before slicing. It can be eaten warm or cold.

# BLINIS / Makes 15–18

When you think of Russia you probably think of vodka, caviar and blinis. And you would be right! These bite-sized little pancakes are a traditional snack and brilliant for serving as canapés. You can choose to top them with various things but soured cream, smoked salmon and maybe a sprinkling of caviar is always a winner. Washed down with a shot of Russian vodka, of course.

**PREP:** 10 minutes

**REST:** 30 minutes

**COOK:** 15 minutes

175ml full-fat milk

80g plain flour

40g buckwheat flour

a pinch of salt

1 teaspoon caster sugar

1 teaspoon instant yeast

1 large egg, separated

vegetable oil, for frying

soured cream and smoked salmon, to serve

1. Heat 125ml of the milk in a saucepan so it's just warm.

2. Place the flours in a mixing bowl. Add the salt, sugar and yeast and stir to combine. Add the warm milk and mix to form a stiff batter. Cover and leave to stand for 30 minutes.

3. Add the egg yolk and the remaining milk to form a thick batter.

4. Whisk the egg white until soft peaks form, then fold into the batter. The batter should be thick, but easily drop off a spoon.

5. Heat a frying pan and lightly oil the base. Add heaped teaspoons of the mixture to the pan and cook until small bubbles appear all over the surface of the blinis. Turn over and cook the other side for about 1 minute until golden brown. Continue to cook in batches until all the batter is used up.

6. Serve with soured cream and smoked salmon.

# MEDOVIK / Serves 4

In mid-eighteenth-century Russia, court cooks avoided using honey in their recipes because the Empress Elizabeth was said to dislike it. However, legend has it that a new young chef arrived in her kitchen and, wanting to impress her, made a layered cake that melted in the mouth. The Empress asked what was in the cake but the young cook was reluctant to say. When he confessed that the main flavour was, in fact, honey, the Empress laughed and the chef was rewarded. Medovik, or honey cake, has remained popular in Russia ever since. Once cooked, leave it to harden up slightly into more of a biscuit texture before assembling the finished layers.

**PREP:** 30 minutes

**BAKE:** 10–12 minutes

**CHILL:** 8 hours or overnight

60g melted unsalted butter

110g honey

110g light soft brown sugar

2 medium eggs

230g plain flour

½ teaspoon baking powder

**for the filling:**

300ml double cream

100ml soured cream

75g icing sugar, sifted

optional: whipped cream, raspberries and crushed honeycomb, to decorate

**equipment:**

43cm x 29cm baking tray

1. Line a 43cm x 29cm baking tray with parchment paper and preheat your oven to 200°C/Gas 6.

2. Mix the melted butter with the honey.

3. In a large bowl, whisk the brown sugar and eggs together until the sugar dissolves. Add the butter and honey and whisk to combine. Add the flour and baking powder and mix to form a thick paste.

4. Spread the mixture into the prepared tray and smooth with a palette knife to level the surface. Make sure this is really even to get perfect layers. Bake for 10 to 12 minutes until golden brown.

5. Remove the cake from the tin and trim the edges to neaten. Whilst still warm, cut into 20 rectangles measuring 5.5cm x 10cm. Leave to go cold and harden.

6. For the filling, whip the double cream until it is thick. Fold in the soured cream and icing sugar.

7. To assemble, take one of the honey biscuit layers and place on a chopping board. Spread with a thin layer of the cream filling Sit another honey biscuit on top and add another layer of filling. Repeat until you have the five layers of biscuit sandwiched with the filling. Leave the top of the cake plain. Repeat using the remaining biscuits until you have four individual honey cakes. Cover and place in the fridge for 8 hours or overnight.

8. The following day the biscuit layers will have softened so a fork slices through easily. You can serve the cakes just as they are or, for a special occasion, pipe with whipped cream and top with fresh raspberries and crushed honeycomb.

# VATRUSHKA / Makes 8

*Vatrushka* is a sweetened yeasted dough bun filled with cheese. It's a typical snack made by Russian families. The girl who served me in a café in St Petersburg recalled learning the recipe from her grandmother and mother. Now she makes them too. If you can't get hold of curd cheese, this recipe works just as well with plain cottage cheese. You can flavour the filling with dried and candied fruit or a little lemon zest.

**PREP:** 25 minutes

**PROVE:** 1¾–3¾ hours

**BAKE:** 15–20 minutes

200–220ml full-fat milk

55g softened unsalted butter, plus extra for greasing

450g strong white bread flour, plus extra for dusting

7g instant yeast

70g caster sugar

a pinch of salt

1 medium egg

1 beaten egg, to glaze

**for the filling:**

110g curd cheese or cottage cheese

110g ricotta

40g caster sugar

1. Place the milk and butter in a small pan and heat gently so the butter melts and the milk is warm.

2. Place the flour in a large bowl, add the yeast to one side and the sugar and salt to the other. Crack the egg into the middle and gradually add three quarters of the warm milk and butter (make sure the milk is warm and not hot). Using your hand, bring the mixture together until a soft dough is formed. Add more milk if the dough is too dry.

3. Tip the dough on to a lightly floured work surface and knead for 5 minutes until you have a smooth dough. Place in a lightly greased bowl, cover and leave to prove until doubled in size. This will take between 1 and 3 hours.

4. Line two baking trays with parchment paper and preheat your oven to 180°C/Gas 4.

5. Tip the dough on to a lightly floured surface and divide into eight equal pieces. Roll each piece into a ball and then, using a rolling pin, roll into a disc approximately 9cm wide. Place the dough discs on the prepared trays, cover and leave to prove for 45 minutes.

6. To make the filling, mix the curd and ricotta cheese with the sugar.

7. Form a hollow in the centre of each dough disc by pressing with a glass. Fill each hollow with the creamy filling. Brush the dough with beaten egg and bake for 15 to 20 minutes in the oven. The dough should be golden and risen around the filling. Cool on a wire rack.

# SWEET BERRY PANCAKES /

Makes 8

Fast-food pancake houses arrived in Russia in 1999. The design and feel of them is the same as the fast-food burger chains we have in the UK. Many types of sweet and savoury pancakes are served, along with the more traditional Russian fare of soups and porridges. Here is my sweet berry pancake recipe with a quick and easy jam. If you haven't used chia seeds before, they act as a natural thickener and give the fruit a jammy consistency.

**PREP:** 30 minutes

**COOK:** 2 minutes
per pancake

**for a quick berry jam:**

100g strawberries

300g raspberries

2 tablespoons chia seeds

30ml orange juice

2 tablespoons runny honey

**for the pancakes:**

155g plain flour

½ teaspoon salt

2 large eggs

190ml full-fat milk

40g melted unsalted butter

sunflower oil, for greasing

soured cream and honey,
to serve

1. To make the berry jam, cut the strawberries in half and put into the bowl of a food processor with all the other ingredients. Blitz until you have a chunky purée that still has a little texture. Taste to check for sweetness and add a little more honey if required. Pour into a bowl or clean jam jar and place in the fridge for about 20 minutes to set.

2. To make the pancakes, place the flour and salt in a mixing bowl. Make a well in the middle and crack the eggs into it. Using a wooden spoon, begin to mix, incorporating the flour from the edge of the bowl.

3. As the mixture thickens, gradually add the milk. Mix well after each addition of milk and continue until all the milk is incorporated and you have a smooth batter. Stir in the melted butter.

4. Place a frying pan at least 20cm in diameter over a medium to high heat. Pour a little oil on to a wad of kitchen paper and lightly wipe the base of the pan to grease it.

5. Pour a little batter (around 3 tablespoons) into the middle of the pan, tip the pan from side to side and swirl the batter round until the base of the pan is covered. Cook for around 30 to 45 seconds, then loosen the edge with a palette knife and flip the pancake over; cook the other side for another 30 to 45 seconds. The pancake should be golden brown.

6. Slide the pancake out of the pan on to greaseproof paper and repeat until all the batter is finished. Stack the pancakes between greaseproof paper until ready to use.

7. To assemble, take a pancake, place a large spoonful of jam in the middle, fold in half, then in half again to make a triangle. Top with soured cream and a drizzle of extra honey.

# DIRECTORY

## MADRID

**Antigua Pastelería del Pozo**
Calle Pozo, 8, 28012 Madrid, Spain

**Chocolatería San Ginés**
Pasadizo San Ginés, 5, 28013 Madrid, Spain
*www.chocolateriasangines.com*

**El Riojano**
Calle Mayor, 10, 28013 Madrid, Spain
*www.confiteriaelriojano.com*

**Horno de San Onofre**
Calle San Onofre, 3, 28004 Madrid, Spain
*www.pasteleriasanonofre.com*

**Viena la Baguette**
Calle de Augusto Figueroa, 24,
28004 Madrid, Spain

## NAPLES

**Antica Pizzeria Port'Alba**
Via Port'Alba, 18, 80134 Naples, Italy

**La Notizia**
Via Michelangelo da Caravaggio, 53
80126 Naples, Italy
*www.pizzarialanotizia.com*

**Pasticceria Capriccio**
Via Pier Santi Mattarella, 106,
91010 San Vito Lo Capo, Italy
*www.pasticceriacapriccio.it*

**Patisserie Capparelli**
Via Tribunali, 325/327,
80138 Naples, Italy

**Pasticceria Pansa**
Piazza Duomo, 40
84011 Amalfi SA, Italy
*www.pasticceriapansa.it*

**Scaturchio**
Piazza San Domenico Maggiore, 19,
80134 Napoli, Italy
*www.scaturchio.it*

## PARIS

**Arnaud Delmontel (various locations)**
39 rue des Martyrs, 75009 Paris, France
*www.arnaud-delmontel.com*

**Laurent Duchêne**
2 rue Wurtz, 75013 Paris, France
*www.laurentduchene.com*

**Liberté**
39 rue des Vinaigriers, 75010 Paris, France
*www.libertepatisserieboulangerie.com*

**Poilâne (various locations)**
8 rue de Cherche-Midi,
75006 Paris, France
*www.poilane.com*

**Du Pain et des Idées**
34 rue Yves Toudic, 75010 Paris, France
*www.dupainetdesidees.com*

**Patisserie Stohrer**
51 rue Montorgueil, 75002 Paris, France
*www.stohrer.fr*

## LONDON

**Bread Ahead**
3 Cathedral St, London SE1 9DE
*www.breadahead.com*

**Cliveden House Hotel**
Cliveden House Hotel, Cliveden Road,
Taplow, Berkshire SL6 0JF
*www.clivedenhouse.co.uk*

**Fortnum & Mason**
181 Piccadilly, London W1A 1ER
*www.fortnumandmason.com*

**Marksman**
254 Hackney Rd, London E2 7SJ
*www.marksmanpublichouse.com*

## COPENHAGEN

**Blomsterbergs**
Toftebæksvej 1,
2800 Kgs. Lyngby, Copenhagen, Denmark
*www.metteblomsterberg.dk*

**Lauras Bakery (various locations)**
Torvehallerne, Linnesgade u/f17,
1361 Copenhagen K, Denmark
*www.laurasbakery.com*

**Meyers Bageri**
Jægersborggade 9,
2200 Copenhagen N, Denmark
*www.meyersmad.dk/spis-ude/meyers-bageri*

**Sankt Peder's Bageri**
Skt Peders Stræde 29,
1453 Copenhagen K, Denmark

**Torvehallerne**
Frederiksborggade 21,
1360 København K, Denmark
*www.torvehallernekbh.dk*

## MUNICH

**Café Frischhut**
Prälat-Zistl-Straße 8, 80331 München,
Germany

**Hofbräuhaus**
Platzl 9, 80331 München, Germany

## NEW YORK

**Dominique Ansel Bakery**
189 Spring St, New York,
NY 10012, United States
*www.dominiqueansel.com*

**Dough Doughnuts**
700 8th Ave, New York,
NY 10036, United States
*www.doughdoughnuts.com*

**Junior's Deli (various locations)**
1515 Broadway, New York,
NY 10019, United States
*www.juniorsrestaurantnewyork.com*

**Murray's Bagels**
500 Ave of the Americas, New York,
NY 10011, United States
*www.murraysbagels.com*

**Sadelle's**
463 W Broadway, New York,
NY 10012, United States
*www.sadelles.com*

**Sullivan St Bakery (various locations)**
533 W 47th St, New York,
NY 10036, United States
*www.sullivanstreetbakery.com*

## MIAMI

**El Brazo Fuerte Bakery**
1697 SW 32nd Ave, Miami,
FL 33145, United States
*www.ebfbakery.com*

**Joe's Stone Crab**
11 Washington Ave, Miami Beach,
FL 33139, United States
*www.joesstonecrab.com*

**Pincho Factory (various locations)**
30 Giralda Ave, Coral Gables,
FL 33134, United States
*pinchofactory.com*

**The Biltmore Hotel**
1200 Anastasia Ave, Coral Gables,
FL 33134, United States
*http://www.biltmorehotel.com*

## WARSAW

**Café Misianka**
Park Skaryszewski, Aleja Waszyngtona,
Warsaw, Poland

**Odette**
07, Wojciecha Górskiego 6,
00-031 Warsaw, Poland

**Piwonski Bakery**
Ul. Warszawska 88, 05-092 Łomianki,
Warsaw, Poland
*www.tradycyjnapiekarnia.pl*

**Pod Barbakanem milk bar**
Mostowa 27, 00-260 Warsaw, Poland

## ST PETERSBURG

**Hotel Astoria**
39 Bolshaya Morskaya, St Petersburg,
190000, Russia,
*www.roccofortehotels.com/hotels-
and-resorts/hotel-astoria*

# INDEX

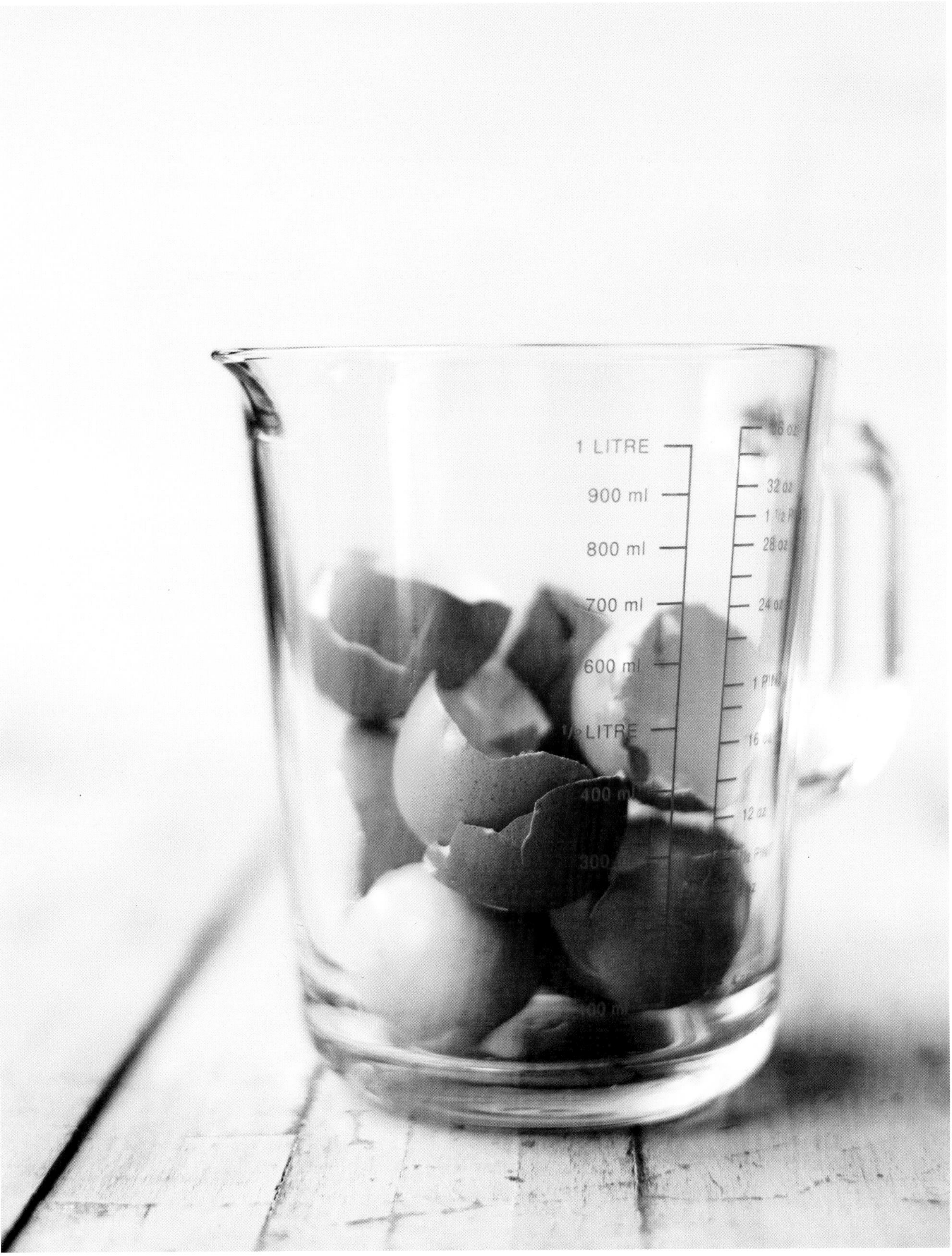
1 LITRE
900 ml
800 ml
700 ml
600 ml
1/2 LITRE
32 oz
28 oz
24 oz
12 oz

# THANKS

This book was inspired by my journey to taste my favourite bakes in the places that they originated. It has been a great adventure and I've had a blast, but I couldn't have done it without some very special people that I'd like to thank:

Alexandra and Josh. My family makes all things possible.

Claire Bassano, who was there throughout the journey and whose dedication and creative input into my recipes is always priceless.

The team at Michael Joseph have been great to work with and have done an amazing job bringing these recipes to life on the page. Special thanks goes to Lindsey Evans, Cookery Publisher, and John Hamilton, Art Director, as well as to the photoshoot gang: Issy Croker for her wonderful photographs, Emma Lahaye for the prop styling and Nikki Morgan and Emma Goodwin who assisted in the kitchen. Thanks also to Zoe Berville, Sophie Elletson and Sarah Fraser in the editorial and design teams at Penguin.

Dunk Barnes and the all the production team at Reef Television involved in my City Bakes programme, which followed my journey.

My agents Geraldine Woods, Kate Cooper and Anna Bruce.